TRUDE HELLER AND G. KEYS
PRESENT

the supremes

lincoln center
PHILHARMONIC HALL
friday, october 15, 1965-- 8:30 pm
mail order and tickets on sale at philharmonic hall $6.80, 6.00, 5.50, 5.00, 4.50, 4.00, 3.50

MARY WILSON *with Mark Bego*

Supreme Glamour

Foreword by
WHOOPI GOLDBERG

348 illustrations

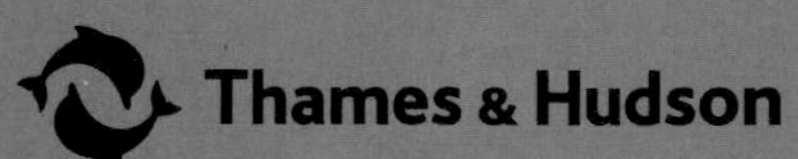

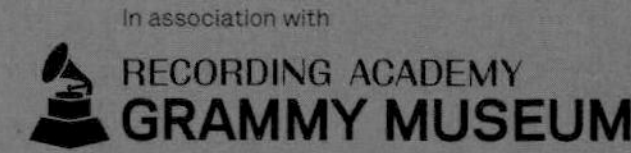

Page 1: Poster designed by Joseph Eula to advertise a performance by The Supremes at the prestigious Lincoln Center Philharmonic Hall, New York, in 1965. Page 2: (L–R) Florence, me and Diane sparkle in the full-length Blue Lagoon gowns we had made in Hong Kong, at this photo shoot from 1966.

Below: Meeting the Queen Mother after the Royal Variety Performance at the London Palladium in London in 1968. We named the gowns "Queen Mother" in memory of the occasion. The show was also attended by Prince Charles and Princess Anne. It was our first command performance, and dashing Engelbert Humperdinck was on the reception line with us.

PRIVA

Below: These form-fitting pink satin gowns with frilly bottoms and a low V neckline both front and back are worn here by (L–R) Diane, me, and Florence during a live performance in c. 1965. They were also worn for some of our most famous publicity shots by James Kriegsmann.

Following page: One of the photos taken for possible use on the cover of our eighth studio album *I Hear a Symphony*, released in 1966.

The inside story of the original pop fashionistas

Diane and I flank Florence in sparkling cream and gold sequin gowns. One of the photographs from the shoot was featured on the cover of the single *"L'amore Verrà"*—the Italian version of "You Can't Hurry Love"—which was released in 1967.

Contents

Foreword

by Whoopi Goldberg

The very first time I ever saw The Supremes, I remember thinking, "Can I ever look like them?" I had a black and white television and I remember seeing them on Ed Sullivan's stage, so poised and elegant. They wore matching tassel dresses and fly shoes, their faces beat and their hair up in a bouffant (except for Flo who had a flip)...they were three of the most beautiful women I had ever seen. Little did I know until much later that the dresses and shoes were salmon color; who knew we could look so good in salmon? And then they opened their mouths, "I've been crying (ooh ooh), cause I'm lonely (for you), smiles have all turned (to tears) but tears won't wash away (the fears)." With arms swaying like thin grass in a mild summer breeze, bodies moving in synchronization, these were brown women as they had never, ever been seen before on national television. The Supremes, right there in front of me, three different shades of brown, gorgeous, stunning, and stylish, made my head explode. Everything about The Supremes—all those gowns, all those pantsuits, all those caps, gloves, furs, the makeup, the eyelashes, the wigs—made me believe they were speaking to me. I too could be well-spoken, tall, majestic, an emissary of black folks, who also came from the projects. Whatever they wore reflected the many looks of black folks, including their hair, which was everything from an Afro to a bob, and that did it for me; that's when I knew I was theirs for life. They were unapologetic and brave. I look back and wonder if they had any idea that they taught me and a new generation the pride of being black. Diana, Mary, and Flo...my heroes.

Whoopi

We perform "Come See About Me" in pale blue short tiered dresses for our first appearance on *The Ed Sullivan Show* in December 1964.

Intro

Dreams do come true

Welcome to my book of dreams! This project has been a labor of love for me, and I hope that everyone around the world is as thrilled as I am with *Supreme Glamour*. On these pages, you will find some of our most famous photographs, as well as countless other images you have never seen before. Yes, it has been said that we were the most famous girl group in musical history; however, in this book, the real stars of the show are the gowns and fashions of The Supremes. "Honey," as Flo would say, "We were the original Dreamgirls." Ha ha! She actually said, "Honey, we is terrific!"

As the original Supremes, Florence Ballard, Diane Ross, and I scored ten No. 1s on the U.S. musical charts. Even after Flo left, we hit No. 1 six more times. Not even our fellow British hit-makers can claim that. Can you imagine our joy when we had our first No. 1 hit, "Where Did Our Love Go"? From that moment on, our career and our fame were magnified and fast-paced. We were so in demand that we constantly had to have more and more exciting high-fashion gowns to wear. Once we grew into the realm of beaded and sequined gowns, the sky was the limit! Feather boas, capes, dresses with butterfly-like wings; we wore it all. In time, our dazzling gowns became as famous as our Motown hits.

I decided to write this book many years ago when I found myself moving from house to house, city to city, and even country to country. I always had to cart boxes of gowns from one storage unit to another. Although I thought I had all of our gowns, after we moved to Los Angeles I realized that many of them were missing. We had originally stored hundreds of gowns at Motown for safekeeping. But when I opened the boxes, I was shocked to discover that along the way many of the dresses had gone missing. Although I had possession of dozens of boxes, I had never stopped to examine the contents. My boxes were always there, waiting to be opened, so how was I to know that some of the contents were missing—even though we had paid for them out of our Supremes account!

In 1988, The Supremes were inducted into the Rock & Roll Hall of Fame. Shortly after, I opened the boxes and took inventory, because I had asked the Hall of Fame Museum to curate the gowns for me. This is when I discovered that hundreds of them were not in my boxes, and I knew then that they had never been returned to us by Motown. However, I had more than enough gowns in my collection at that time to be exhibited in the U.S.A. and the U.K. While I was still searching for the missing items, and even finding some on eBay, I presented an exhibition of my gowns in several museums, and people are still flocking to see them. They truly are works of art and should be seen.

Now, at long last, I am presenting to you my coffee table book *Supreme Glamour*. It is all about our career, our exciting accomplishments, and our glamorous gowns, which we wore all over the world.

In this book, you will see for yourself just how many fashion statements we made, even though there were no red carpets or fashion television shows back then. Both on stage and off stage, there were many fashion trends we personified. What we wore truly mattered. We took our fans from the sophisticated shirtwaist dresses of

Here I am wearing my "Goldie" dress, shown on page 118, in a portrait photograph taken in 1968.

the 1950s, to the go-go boots and elaborate hairpieces/wigs and gowns of the 1960s, to the Afros and "hot pants" of the disco 1970s, and beyond. We were so iconic that we had our own brand of bread and our own wig line. Our audiences always anticipated what we were going to wear on our next television performance, concert, or nightclub appearance. I hope we never disappointed them! The purpose of this book is to show the beauty and style of The Supremes. It is a style that is copied by millennials today.

The Supremes' "brand" started more than fifty years ago in Detroit, Michigan. At that time, we were "Primettes," back when rock 'n' roll was still new. Florence Ballard, Diana Ross, Betty McGlown-Travis, and I first became The Primettes when three guys named The Primes and their manager, Milton Jenkins, decided that they wanted to put together a package to make a show. Although The Supremes found fame as a trio, there were four of us in the beginning, and three of us were only thirteen years old. Betty, the fourth girl, was a few years older.

In the beginning, we wore simple pleated skirts and sweaters with Oxford shoes. We looked so naïve and innocent back then. However, we quickly moved up to wearing cheap pearls that we bought from the Woolworth's "five & dime" store downtown on Woodward Avenue. Those pearls may have been faux, but when I wore them they made me feel even more sophisticated, confident, and grown up.

Not long afterward, we advanced to wearing short homemade dresses. Diane and I made outfits using Butterick patterns. Diane was better at this than I was because she attended Cass Technical High School, which had college degree courses, whereas I had the regular "home economics" classes from Northeastern High School on the east side of Detroit. My mom was a domestic worker and had been given a sewing machine by a white family; me and Diane sewed up a storm. My Aunt Moneva helped us make the dresses when Betty left us and Barbara Martin joined the group. My aunt was so good at sewing that she could even make hats and coats.

Although many books have been written about The Primettes/The Supremes, this is the first official coffee table book of our rise to fame, from beginning to end, written by an original founding member—me, Mary Wilson. This book is our beautiful, glittering, and "glamorous" career in pictures. In the chaotic world of today, I think we all need some glamour in our lives. In *Supreme Glamour,* I am going to give it to you!

How did three little black teenage girls from Detroit, Michigan, become the most beloved and biggest-selling female singing trio in music history? It came down to one mutual thing that we had in our hearts: we "Dared to Dream."

"Touch"

Mary Wilson

Dreamgirls to fashionistas

1959 to 1965

It all began in June 1959 when Florence, Diane, Betty, and I formed The Primettes. I was a fifteen-year-old schoolgirl when we gave our first performance at a Local 49 social in Detroit later that year, and only sixteen when we signed to Motown as The Supremes in January 1961. For a while, we were the "no hit Supremes," but in 1964 we finally had a №. 1 single—"Where Did Our Love Go"—and after that the hits kept on coming. With success came glamorous gowns, live tours of the U.S.A. and Europe, and many television performances.

Below: Flo (center) and I attend Betty's wedding at her house in Detroit in 1959. Diane most likely took this picture.
Bottom: As The Primettes (L–R), Betty, me, Flo, and Diane styled ourselves with pearls and button earrings.

The early years

1959 to 1964

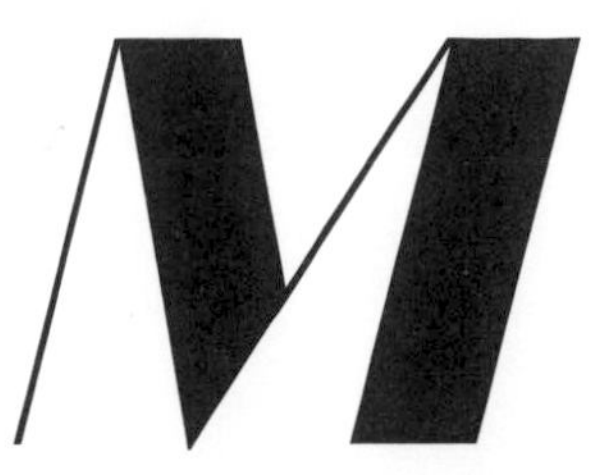y first singing group, The Primettes, formed in 1959 when I was fifteen years old and living in Detroit. It was the era when groups such as The Platters, The Drifters, The Coasters, The Flamingos, the incredible Fats Domino, and Little Richard were the hot recording acts. In 1958, I had moved to Bishop Elementary School, which was across the street from the Brewster-Douglass public housing project where I lived. Detroit schools had great arts departments at that time, and they encouraged singing and performing, too. When an amateur talent night was announced at Bishop Elementary, I knew I wanted to take part. I signed up for the show, and almost immediately began rehearsing to a recording of Frankie Lymon & The Teenagers' hit "I'm Not A Juvenile Delinquent" (1956), which was featured in the movie *Rock, Rock, Rock!* (1956).

I decided to not only sing the song, but also to adopt the look and swagger that Frankie Lymon & The Teenagers delivered in the film. To accomplish this, I tied a "do-rag" on my head and tried to emulate the stance of a streetwise delinquent. Although I was pretty square myself, living in the projects meant that I definitely knew a lot of delinquents.

In the school auditorium, once I started my performance, the song seemed to flow out of me. I delivered a passionate rendition, and when I finished my teenage audience erupted into an enthusiastic round of hooting, hollering, and applause. I was so excited; my heart was pounding. Being on stage in front of an audience was like being in heaven. I still have that same feeling whenever I perform now, some sixty years later.

Instead of returning to the audience, I watched the rest of the students perform from the side of the stage. Also singing at the talent show that night was a pretty girl I had seen in my neighborhood. Her name was Florence Ballard, and she was one of the singers who performed after me. I was instantly impressed with her engaging streetwise elegance. Flo had big brown eyes and she was very fair-skinned; in the black community she was what people called "high yellow." And, she had a lovely heart-shaped face and a beautiful light mane of hair. Because of the slightly golden color of her hair, she earned the nickname "Blondie." Florence sang her operatic version of the song "Ave Maria" without music (a cappella), and received a huge round of applause when she finished. The two of us congratulated each other on our performances, hugging and jumping up and down as teenage girls are prone to do. After the show, we walked home together, and amid our conversation, we made a vow to each other. Florence and I promised that if either of us heard about a singing group that we could join, we would tell the other one.

One day, a few weeks later, Florence came running up to me in the school hallway with a huge smile on her face. Excitedly grabbing my arm she asked, "Mary, do you want to be in a singing group with me and two other girls?"

A local male singing group called The Primes wanted to form a female singing group. Flo's sister, Maxine Ballard, was dating The Primes' very charismatic manager, Milton Jenkins, at the time, and she told him about Flo, which is how the opportunity came about. The Primes were a singing trio that comprised Eddie Kendricks, Paul Williams, and Kell Osborne.

Paul was dating a girl by the name of Betty McGlown-Travis at the time, and Milton was convinced she would be perfect for the group he was envisioning. One of the guys had also asked another girl, Diane Ross, who lived across the street from me to join the group. I did not know Diane at that time, but I had seen her from my bedroom window, playing with the boys. She was thin like me and very cute.

At this particular time, there was a brief craze for male singing groups and female singing groups to be billed together as "brother" and "sister" acts. Milton explained that it was his idea to create a girl group to perform on the same bill as The Primes. According to Florence, Milton wanted to call us The Primettes and he wanted to start rehearsing immediately. I instantly loved the idea.

There was only one obstacle; I had to get my mother's permission. I remember excitedly announcing to her, "Mama! Mama! Can I join this singing group? It's called The Primettes. Please!?! Please, please, please?"

She looked at me and said, "The Primates?"

"No, The Primettes. My friend Flo says The Primes are looking for a sister group, so she asked me to join the group."

Since I was a young pretty teenager, my mother was concerned that I would get into mischief with local boys, or some sort of trouble. She ultimately figured that singing with a group of girls was a good way for me to spend my after-school time.

Florence and I made plans to meet up with our new friend Diane and go to visit Milton and The Primes later that day. We three walked the few blocks, getting to know each other on the way as we headed toward the apartment building of the local hotel where Milton lived. It was right down the street from the Flame Show Bar, which was located at Canfield Street and John R. This was one of Detroit's most famous nightclubs. Everyone played there, from Billie Holiday and Dinah Washington, to B.B. King, Etta James, and the Nat King Cole Trio.

Maurice King, who later was one of our mentors in the artist development department at Motown, was the band leader there. Obviously, we were too young to go into bars at that time, but once John Oden—an assistant to Berry Gordy—took us there during the day to meet Sam Cooke, while he was rehearsing.

Actually, all three members of The Primes were currently living with Milton in his apartment at the hotel. When we got there, we met Betty McGlown-Travis, who was to be the fourth girl in the group. As The Primettes—Betty, Flo, Diane, and I—instantly meshed together, not only vocally but as friends as well. This was suddenly so exciting! Had our parents known that we were going to Milton's "bachelor apartment," they would have freaked out, because we were still only teenagers.

We also met Janie Bradford there, who later co-wrote the hit "Money (That's What I Want)" (1959) with Berry Gordy. She was dating The Primes' Kell Osborne, and over time we all became lifelong friends. This included Paul Williams and Eddie Kendricks, who went on to form The Temptations.

That afternoon, we were extremely impressed by how very polished and sophisticated and handsome The Primes were. After the guys showed off some of their favorite songs, we girls sang several songs, including Hank Ballard's "The Twist," The Drifters' "There Goes My Baby," and "(Night Time) Is The Right Time" (all 1959) by Ray Charles with The Raylettes. Since Betty didn't live in our neighborhood, I didn't get the chance to hang out with her as often as I did with Diane and Flo. Because Flo, Diane, and I spent so much time together, I felt that they "completed" me. Between the three of us, and our different characters—Flo's streetwise personality and Diane's perpetually outgoing drive—we became a perfect unit. Together, we were like one complete woman.

For months, we rehearsed every day at Milton's apartment, and finally we were about to get our first major gig. One day, when we were hanging out of the window at Milton's, we saw a guy walk by with a guitar. I realized that I knew him from school, and we asked him if he could play the guitar he had on his back. He looked up and said, "Yes I can." So we said, "Come on up." And that is how we met our fifth Primette, Marv Tarplin. For a time, he was our guitar player and an important part of the band.

For our first gig, we were booked to perform at a party for one of the big Detroit automotive unions. I believe it was a Local 49. There was going to be a lot of influential people there, and for us it was an important performance. We dressed in our trademark identical outfits, which Milton had asked one of his many girlfriends to buy for us. That night, we wore white pleated skirts and white sweaters, each with a large "P" sewn on the front to stand for "Primettes." Our outfits were completed with matching white socks and white Oxford shoes.

The performance was a huge success. Milton was our manager, and he really believed in us. We were very well taken care of: he would have one of his ladies take us shopping and would drive us to and fro in his red Cadillac convertible. Every time he came to the projects to pick us up, everyone would peer out of their windows to watch. We were already being treated like stars by Milton.

Not long after that, Diane and I decided to make some of our dresses ourselves. One day, we went downtown to purchase fabric and a pattern for the dresses. We cut them out of a colorful orange and yellow fabric and sewed them together. The bodices were tight at the waist; the dress then ballooned out at the hips, and came in at the knee. The balloon look was very "in vogue" then, and even now. These were our first formal stage outfits, and for us, at the time, wearing them made us feel like we were at the peak of high fashion.

After the Local 49 party, we continued to polish our act by doing other local gigs. It was

The Primettes wear homemade dresses sewn by Diane and me, with the help of my Aunt Moneva (1961). By this time, Betty had left to focus on her marriage and Barbara Martin (left) had joined us.

the era of big teenage dances, and what were known as "sock hops" and "record hops." These were dances held in high school gymnasiums and ballrooms, and the kids would take off their shoes and dance in their socks. In Detroit, and all over the country, "sock hops" were all the craze back then. I loved looking down from the stage and watching kids our own age dancing and having a great time while we sang.

Finally, we got our big break at the Detroit, Michigan/Windsor, Ontario, annual International Freedom Festival held on July 4, 1960. Marv Tarplin played guitar, which made us stand out from the other acts. Florence, Diane, Betty, and I were so determined to win our first contest.

We were literally jumping for joy when the winning act's name was announced: "The Primettes." We were excited beyond belief! I mean every act was good, and very different. Oscar Huckabee, an exotic dancer, was fabulous, and this was before gay or trans people performed widely, despite "gay liberation" being only a few years away. Plus, there were doo-wop groups, a ventriloquist, and juggling acts. But, it was The Primettes who won the international prize that day.

In addition to the honor of winning first prize, we were given $15.00, a huge amount to us at the time. I was elected to take care of the money—well, maybe I elected myself. However, after several hours of us touring the festival and enjoying the rides, when it came time to divide up the prize money, I discovered that I had somehow lost the cash. It must have happened while we were on the rides. I don't think the girls believed me, but I felt so sorry.

By this point, we were starting to hear the music of Motown coming out of radios all over town. The first Motown record that was played like crazy was Barrett Strong's "Money (That's What I Want)" (1959). Eddie Holland, Marv Johnson, Mabel John, Henry Lumpkin, Richard "Popcorn" Wylie, and The Miracles were also among the first Motown hit-makers we heard.

Fueled by the confidence of our triumphant win at the International Freedom Festival, we realized that we too needed to record. That's when we "dared to dream—big!"

Diane told us that she knew Smokey Robinson's cousin Sylvia, and that she would try to reach out to her about getting an audition for The Primettes. As the lead singer and prime songwriter of The Miracles, Smokey was the reigning golden boy at Motown. Other members of the group were Pete Moore, Ronnie White, Bobby Rogers, and his cousin Claudette Rogers. Diane told Sylvia about us, and as it all came together, we were told to meet at Claudette's house. At the audition, The Miracles were impressed by what they saw and heard from us. However, the bad thing that came about from this meeting was that they were really impressed with Marv Tarplin's guitar playing and they liked him. So, that was the day we lost our guitarist and the fifth Primette.

Shortly after auditioning for The Miracles, we got our audition with Berry Gordy Jr. We were so excited! Berry Gordy and his fledgling Motown Records were already becoming legends. We wanted our big chance there, too.

Our audition came in the late summer of 1960. I remember arriving at the legendary two-story house known as "Hitsville U.S.A.," which was Motown's headquarters. There was a banner outside that read: "The Sound of Young America." It made everything seem so enticing and so within our reach, as we were—after all—young and American. We stepped into the offices and there sat Janie Bradford. She had gone from dating one of The Primes to become the receptionist at Motown.

The Primettes sat in the tiny waiting room for what felt like an eternity. Finally, we were taken into the studio and introduced to Robert Bateman, Richard Morris, and the man himself: Mr. Berry Gordy Jr. He had a businesslike air about him, which commanded respect. Both Robert and Richard were songwriters at Motown. Robert later became well-known as one of the writers of The Marvelettes' big hit "Please Mr. Postman" (1961). Richard was very nice to us during the audition, and gave us cues to start and stop. They wanted to hear our voices and how they blended, so we sang a cappella. That day at Hitsville we sang our hearts out. If this was going to be our big break, we had to give it our all.

Mr. Gordy seemed impressed, but when we finished he told us to come back after we had graduated from high school. We were all stunned, but that was the edict that was handed to us. Naturally, we were disappointed. However, looking back at that era, I can now see what Mr. Gordy's true motivation was. He simply did not want to be responsible for a group of young teenage girls.

Below: This is the first professional photograph of The Supremes after we signed to Motown in 1961. I never liked it much as I thought we looked much cuter in person. Bottom: Promotional art for "Let Me Go The Right Way" (1962). It was produced by Berry Gordy and was one of the first singles we released as a trio.

Below: Fans line up in the rain to see their favorite Motown stars on tour in the Motortown Revue (1963).
Bottom: The "no hit Supremes," (L-R) Florence, me, and Diane, perform at the Apollo Theater, New York, in 1963.

Being young, we didn't understand that at the time. All we understood was that we did not get into Motown.

The funny thing was that none of the four of us girls had any intention of not graduating from high school. We all came from good homes, we prized our educations, and our diplomas were as important to us as being signed to a recording label. Plus, our parents would have killed us had we not graduated, because at that time in the black community, parents saw it as paramount that their children got an education.

On our way out of Hitsville, I recall Flo saying about Mr. Gordy, "He can't be that great, if he can't tell how good we are!" Even though we had been turned down by Motown, Richard Morris ran up to us and said, "Hey girls, guess what? I know of another record label that might be interested in you. They are called Lupine Records."

It was around this time that Betty told us that she was leaving the group to get married. Losing Betty was hard on Flo, because the two of them had become very close. Meanwhile, Diane and I had also become close and we shared everything. We would call each other and talk and talk in those days. Even though in later life people think I was closer to Flo, in truth it was Diane and I who were always more alike, and close.

As we only had three Primettes now, Richard brought in Barbara Randolph and Betty Kendrick to fill out our sound. The most well-known singer on Lupine Records was Wilson Pickett, and we sung backgrounds for a couple of his recordings when he was part of the group The Falcons. There were also seven or eight other records we sang on at Lupine, including background vocals for Eddie Floyd. These recordings weren't released until years later. As The Primettes, we recorded several songs for Lupine, including "Tears of Sorrow" and "Pretty Baby" (both 1960). We were never paid.

Suddenly that summer, Diane and I did not hear from Flo for several weeks. We were terrified. We called her on the phone, but her family would not let us see or talk with her for almost a month. Diane and I just couldn't imagine what had made our friend not want to speak to us anymore. When she finally contacted us, Flo told us the horrifying news that she had been sexually molested by a local guy. Hearing the whole ugly story was like being in a nightmare. As teenage girls, we could not possibly know what Florence had been going through. Being turned down by Mr. Gordy was heartbreaking, naturally, but Flo's tragedy was by far the worst thing we had ever encountered.

There was no one there to help Florence get through her ordeal. In those days, no one talked about such things. No wonder her family would not let us see her; they must have been out of their minds with grief. Today, we have the "Me Too" movement and numerous outlets to help young girls and boys who have gone through these types of degrading experiences. People now feel more able to come forward to tell their stories of rape and abuse, without shame. However, back then Flo simply had to live quietly with her emotional scars. The damage had been done.

Although Flo came back to the group, she was never the same carefree, cheeky girl she had been before. She kept everything inside. It was like the Jimmy Webb song I later recorded and sang to Flo called "I Keep It Hid" (1972).

After a difficult series of events—being turned down by Motown, losing Betty, and Florence's tragedy—we decided to go back to Motown, where there was hope. Lupine was a good recording experience for us, but we wanted to resume our quest to get signed by Motown Records. To accomplish this goal, we camped out in front of Hitsville every day, hoping to get inside. We would do anything to get our feet in the door.

We watched Mary Wells walk up the sidewalk, and we warmly greeted her with a charming, "Hello Mary!" Or when one or more of The Miracles came up the sidewalk, we would shout out, "Hello Pete! Hello Bobby!" or "Hello Ron! Hello Claudette!" We became a regular fixture there, and we did everything we could to ingratiate ourselves to the Motown stars as they walked by.

What a big surprise it was to see our friends Paul Williams and Eddie Kendricks of The Primes with Otis Williams of The Distants walking up to Hitsville one day. We had lost touch with Milton Jenkins, so we chatted and caught up with each other. Another friend, Melvin Franklin of The Distants, asked, "Where is Betty?"

We told him that we had lost Betty, and that she had gone off to get married. Then we added that we were looking for a fourth girl.

"I know of the perfect girl for you!" Melvin said. "Her name is Barbara Martin."

Melvin quickly set up a meeting at the Graystone Ballroom. Barbara was so pretty

We perform for a teenage audience in 1962 at one of the many "record hops" we played in Detroit before we became recording artists. By that time, Barbara Martin was pregnant and had already left to get married.

and charming that evening; we instantly loved her, and thought she was the perfect fourth member for The Primettes. We knew we had made the right choice, because Barbara was not only a great-looking girl, but she was also tall and very cute, and so much fun, too!

We were all so cute back then. But being cute alone was not going to help us get a hit record. We had to get into the recording studio and have the opportunity to sing and show Hitsville our trademark harmonies. Now the four of us were determined to be signed to Motown Records, we could not be deterred. After months of hanging around, at last one of the producers come out and said, "We need some hand claps on a track we're working on." We excitedly jumped at the opportunity and replied in unison, "We'll do it!"

After we eventually made our way into Hitsville, we became such fixtures there that Mr. Gordy and everyone else just referred to us as "the girls." We would literally follow Mr. Gordy around from room to room, hoping we would get the chance to record.

One of Mr. Gordy's sisters had her own record company in Detroit called Anna Records. While Mr. Gordy was launching Motown, Anna had signed some great stars to her label, including The Contours and Harvey & The Moonglows, and one of the members of The Moonglows was Marvin Gaye. When Anna Records closed its doors, these artists came over to Motown Records. That was the first time we met Marvin Gaye. I will never forget him coming to Hitsville; he was just so handsome! All of us girls were swooning over him back then.

At last we were in, and it seemed that we did backgrounds for everybody. We were so happy to be in anyone's recording session that we didn't care what the part was. Whatever they wanted on a session, we were happy to supply. We sang the background parts on records by Mary Wells, and in time we even sang with Marvin Gaye on some of his hits, such as "Can I Get A Witness" (1963) and "You're A Wonderful One" (1964). This was before The Rayber Voices—or later The Andantes—were on hand as the in-house background singers.

Diane even took a part-time job at Hitsville as Berry's assistant, or created one for herself! In fact, many artists assumed various jobs. Even Martha Reeves would later do the same thing, creating a job for herself as producer Mickey Stevenson's assistant. One day, when there was a need for a background session in the studio and the regular background singers were nowhere to be found, Martha recommended her group The Vels, who later became The Vandellas. That is just how Motown was back then.

It has been said that Motown made us over. However, as young girls, when we went to Motown we already had our own sense of style. Our families and our church gave us this. Did Motown mold us into the fashion icons that we were later credited as being? They certainly nurtured it and encouraged it, but in reality, one of the things that impressed them the most when we arrived there was our chic look and our strong sense of classy style.

While we were having fun being in the studio, we were also meeting all the people as they came in. I remember the day Stevie Wonder arrived at Hitsville. Mr Gordy had said to us that he was seeing a nine-year-old genius that day. I especially remember wanting to see what a "genius" looked like. Flo, Diane, and I looked on as Stevie jumped from musical instrument to instrument; he was able to play them all. I was really impressed. Mr. Gordy's eyes were as wide as can be, watching in awe as Stevie demonstrated what being a "musical genius" was all about.

In 1961, when our big chance came, it was the happiest day of my life. This was the day we were to sign our recording contract with Motown Records. When Mr. Gordy asked, "Do you have a new name?", it was like he had dropped a bomb on us. I felt that it was a real game changer, but did not know why. The first thing that went through my mind was, "No one is gonna know us if we change our name from The Primettes!" However, I knew we would have to come up with something new if we were to sign a recording contract with Motown. Mr. Gordy had asked us to change our name before, but who knew he had been serious? We each had asked every one we knew in school, at church, our family, and friends, but it was our good buddy Janie Bradford who came through for us in the end. She had a small brown paper bag, and lots of names had been put into it. Flo took control and pulled out "The Supremes."

Flo said, "I choose The Supremes." That was it! I certainly didn't like the name at first, as it sounded too much like a building. In those days, groups always chose names because of gender. Girl groups almost always put "-ells" or "-ettes" at the end of their names to sound more "girlie," such as The Ikettes, The Raelettes, or The Primettes. But Flo made the executive decision, and we were now officially "The Supremes." That's when we were given our contracts.

We were all still minors, so our mothers had to sign for us, too. My mother could not read nor write, but I don't think any of us actually read a damn word on that piece of paper that day. Had we done so, we might have seen that somewhere in there it stated that Motown owned any fictitious name that we used. We really should have had a lawyer, but who had the money? Plus, we trusted Berry completely, and felt we did not need a lawyer. Only years later, when Flo was put out of the group, did I read the contract. However, at the time, I would have signed away my grandchildren for the opportunity we were being given.

We were so excited just to be there and recording. We were living in the moment, being teenage girls in the recording studio. We loved it!

The four of us recorded dozens of songs. Barbara is on every one of the songs featured on our album *Meet The Supremes* (1962). You can hear her on the song "He's Seventeen," doing the whole dialogue piece in the middle, where she says, "Guess what girls?" and we reply, "Whaaat?" "I'm seventeen!" We all laughed so much while we were recording that song because it was so funny. We were truly happy being with each other.

On the song "Those D.J. Shows," we found some of Smokey Robinson's sentence structure to be ridiculously funny. After we sang it, the four of us ran out of the studio laughing hysterically at the crazy lyrics in the song. It was great fun to record with Diane, Barbara, and Flo. We were "besties" for life. We just had so much fun in the recording studio back then. Those were some of the best moments of my life! We bonded so much during this era.

Our first single as The Supremes was "I Want A Guy" (1961), with Diane on lead. It was written by Berry Gordy and Freddie Gorman. Freddie was a member of a group called The Originals. At the time, he was also our mailman! The first time we heard "I Want A Guy" on local radio station WCLB, we were thrilled. We finally had a record out, and it was a "dream come true" for all of us.

Our second single, "Buttered Popcorn" (1961), had Florence singing the lead, and the way she sang it was very playful and so much fun. These first two singles were on the Tamla label.

"Buttered Popcorn" was written by Berry Gordy and Barney Ales. Everyone thought that Motown was an all-black record company, but Barney and many others on Motown's sales staff were white. Barney ran the sales department, and we all really liked him because he was so "real." He and Mr. Gordy were close friends also.

Barney wrote the lyrics to the song "Buttered Popcorn" after he and his wife had been to the movies, together with Mr. Gordy and his wife, Raynoma. When Barney asked his wife what she had got for him to eat, she replied, "Popcorn." When he asked her if she put butter on it, she told him "Yes," and he kept saying, "More butter, more butter, more," because he liked his popcorn with a whole lot of butter on it. That became the basis of the song's theme.

For The Supremes, single after single was released, but somehow none of them became hits. At first, we had just wanted to sing, then we had wanted to be at Motown and to record. Now we desperately wanted a hit record.

But we were graduating from high school at the time , and we had to decide what we were going to do. Get a job? Apply to college? Or, release a hit record? New artists were coming into Motown and scoring their first hits: The Marvelettes, The Four Tops, and The Vandellas. We watched as these new acts began to get all the attention. I can see now that many of the other acts felt the same way when we later got our first hit. I can honestly say that we all loved each other, but at Motown, whoever got the hit record got all of the attention. All of a sudden we were in a whole new mindset. It was like that key moment in the movie *Sunset Boulevard* (1950), "Yes, we, The Supremes, are ready for our close-up now!"

We watched from the sidelines as Mary Wells became more and more successful. She had her first hit, "Bye Bye Baby," at the beginning of 1961, and she had a streak of three Top 10 hits in a row. Then Motown signed a new female group, The Marvelettes. We were in the studio with them when Gladys Horton started having some trouble singing her lead vocals. Florence stepped in and gave her a few tips, which shows how we really were a family of artists at Motown.

Below: Florence, Diane, and me in the recording studio at Hitsville in January 1965.
Bottom: A record store in New York fills its window display with hits by The Supremes to celebrate the group's third No. 1 single in a row (1964).

When The Marvelettes hit No. 1 with "Please Mr. Postman" in 1961, on both the pop and the R&B charts, they were suddenly treated like conquering heroines. Martha & The Vandellas came along in 1963 and began with three instant hits: "Come And Get These Memories," "Heat Wave," and "Quicksand." Then another trio, The Velvelettes, scored their big hit "Needle in a Haystack" (1964).

We were no longer "the girls." Other "girls" were now at Motown, and since we weren't producing hit records I thought we were quickly being eclipsed in everyone's eyes. We watched as The Temptations and The Four Tops had their first hit records in early 1964, and suddenly they too were treated like "stars" at the company.

I was afraid that everyone at Motown was laughing behind our backs. In my imagination I wondered if they were thinking, "Those poor Supremes. They can't seem to get a hit record." This was when I created my own term for the dilemma we found ourselves in. I called us "the no hit Supremes." It was exactly what I felt like, and it defined what we were at the time.

Before we ultimately found success, several more changes occurred. Around this time, Barbara told us that she was leaving the group to get married. We were disappointed to see her go, but we decided to continue as a trio.

Knowing that we were struggling to score a hit recording, Mr. Gordy said, "We've got to get the girls a hit record." That is when he put us together with his top writing team: Brian Holland, Lamont Dozier, and Eddie Holland. They became known simply as "Holland-Dozier-Holland," and they were also known at the company as "H-D-H."

They composed the song "When The Lovelight Starts Shining Through His Eyes" (1963), and recording it was a thrill unto itself. It was an exciting up tempo song, and we thought we finally had a hit record on our hands. Our recording made it to No. 23 on the *Billboard* Hot 100 chart. It was a huge breakthrough for us, and we were ecstatic.

Then in March of 1964 came our next single, "Run, Run, Run." We thought this was going to be an even bigger hit, but it barely made the *Billboard* charts, where it peaked at No. 93.

Next, Holland-Dozier-Holland said to us, "We have just come up with some 'smashes' for you!" When we heard "Where Did Our Love Go" (1964), none of us were really excited about it. I remember saying to Eddie Holland, "If we don't get a hit record, our parents are going to make us go to college. He said, "Trust me Mary, this song is going to be a real big hit." The main reason that we did not care for "Where Did Our Love Go" was that we wanted a song more like the other groups had. We wanted more R&B-driven rhythms like the latest hits by The Marvelettes, The Temptations, and Martha & The Vandellas.

When we started as the quartet "The Primettes," we sang such great harmonies together. We came from the doo-wop era of music, when harmonies were "the thing." Everything we did was surrounded in harmony, and "Where Did Our Love Go" didn't have any of that. It was a "basic" song with a basic beat. However, Holland-Dozier-Holland insisted that we record it. Plus we were pretty low down on the totem pole at the company at this point. We couldn't say, "Oh, no, we're not doing it." We had to accept it, as we were still—according to my phrase—"the no hit Supremes."

It was at this time that Mr. Gordy told us that he wanted Diane to be the lead singer. Diane's singing style was perfect for it. As long as one of us was chosen we did not care which one. The main thing for us is that we got a hit record. We just wanted a hit. I know that people think that Flo and I were upset, but that is not true. Another rumor that is not true is that the song "Where Did Our Love Go" was given to The Marvelettes first. Eddie Holland told me that it was specifically written for us, The Supremes.

Perhaps this is a good time to point out that even though I would wake up singing and was in every music class in school, I never thought of myself as a singer per se. It has always been being up on stage that has excited me the most. As much as I cared about singing, I also loved the dancing, the comedy bits, the choreography, and engaging a live audience. Performing is still my real gift and my real love. I am an entertainer; Diane and Flo were "the singers."

When we started recording with Holland-Dozier-Holland, it was like working with three professors: these guys were pros. The great thing about Holland-Dozier-Holland writing and producing our songs was that they had really dissected it before they gave it to you. They knew what they wanted to do; it was not up to us. Lamont and Brian worked on the lyrics. Then they worked with Flo and I on the backing parts, while

Below: Diane takes the lead while Florence and I sing background vocals on stage in 1964. I have no clue whose idea it was to put those huge white bows on our heads —to this day I dislike bows.

Bottom: Diane, Florence, and I perform in concert in 1964. In the early days at record hops we wore our signature chiffony short dresses. We had them in salmon, pink and these beautiful green three-tiered versions. I loved the crystal ball necklaces.

Eddie worked with Diane on the lead. The song was already broken down: who sings what, and how we sing it.

When we recorded the song, my voice was closer to the microphone, because Florence's was so strong and they needed more softness, a more mellow voice dominating. On the recording of "Where Did Our Love Go", you can hear more of my voice, but you can also feel Florence's soul underneath it. Diane was naturally higher, so Eddie had her sing down a register, which gave her a sexier sound. Once Flo and I started recording the song, we totally got into it. Eddie said that Diane was uncomfortable singing in a lower register, but at the end of the recording he was very satisfied with her performance.

It was Eddie Holland who gave all of the lead singers their vocal approach. I wish I'd had the opportunity to have him teach me how to sing, too, because I stopped growing as a singer. I watched Diane improve her vocals on each session, while both Flo and I stayed the same. It was especially sad for Flo. I started noticing her disappointment about not singing "out front" at this early stage, but she never complained. I grew much more on stage than I did in the recording studio, as I enjoyed the freedom of no one stopping me while I was performing.

Little did we know at the time we recorded "Where Did Our Love Go" that it was going to mark such a major change for The Supremes. We had no idea that this one song was going to immediately define the sound and the vocal appeal of the group.

Although every time we recorded a song we were praying for a hit record, this one felt different from the very start. How can one explain the extraordinary enduring appeal of "Where Did Our Love Go"? I don't know if I have a definitive answer. However, it gave us our first of sixteen No. 1 records. People were playing it all over the world. Even NASA beamed it up to astronauts Gordon Cooper and Pete Conrad on Gemini 5 as they orbited around Earth!

When that song was first released, we were on the road performing on that year's annual Dick Clark's "Caravan of Stars" tour. We were on the bill with some very well-known acts, including Gene Pitney, The Shirelles, Cliff Richard, The Drifters, The Crystals, and my favorite group, The Dixie Cups. When we started the tour, Mr. Clark would introduce us on stage and we would receive almost no hand claps of recognition from the audience. No one knew us. We had not been on national television yet. In fact, Dick Clark had asked his booking agent, Liz Ross, to contact Motown to book Brenda Holloway. When she called, Liz was told, "If you want Brenda, you have to take The Supremes, too."

It was while we were on the tour that "Where Did Our Love Go" was released, and it became a bigger hit week by week. We literally became stars while we were on that tour. Each night, when Dick Clark announced "The Supremes," the applause got progressively louder and louder. Then, one night, we heard people screaming and yelling for us when they announced our names. We didn't know what was going on! I thought that Gene Pitney had stuck his head out from behind the curtain, but actually it was because our song had become No. 1 in the country. We had no idea how fast it had climbed up the charts and that we had our first chart-topping hit.

When we flew home to Detroit, we felt like we were bona fide stars. Plus, it was our first plane ride—"Yeah!"—which was exciting in itself. Now that we had found stardom at last, we expected to go back to Motown and find that there were big paychecks with our names on them.

We had surely seen Motown become a huge power in the music industry, and we had witnessed people around us finding sudden wealth. For example, all of the songwriters—Smokey Robinson, William Stevenson, and of course Holland-Dozier-Holland—were now driving expensive shiny new cars, because of all the money they had suddenly made. Some days, it looked like a Cadillac dealership showroom in front of Motown.

I elected myself as the spokesperson for the group, and I went to Esther Edwards' office at Motown expecting to find checks made out to me, Diane, and Flo. Well, I was certainly in for a rude awakening!

Anyone who knows how the record business works would know that the real money is made by the record company, and the songwriters. It is the songwriters at Jobete Music who get paid a huge royalty whenever a Motown song is played on the radio. The singers get nothing from radio airplay. What recording artists receive is a percentage of actual record sales. I did not know how the business worked, but since we had just gotten a hit record and sold a million copies of

We give a polished performance on the TV show *Shindig!* (1964), where we sang "Baby Love" and "Come See About Me." At this point, our style is still au naturel.

We pose for a group portrait in 1964, wearing the simple two-piece designs we wore on *Shindig!* This image was used on the cover of an eighteen-track "Classic" compilation album released in 2008.

This photo from 1964 shows us wearing a boat-neck lace top over a figure-hugging full-length dress. An image from this photo shoot was included in *Meet The Supremes*, a biographical booklet published by Motown in 1965.

Fans line up to see us in concert at The Cave nightclub in Vancouver, Canada. The venue was well known for hosting world-class acts, including Fats Domino, Ella Fitzgerald, Tina Turner, and James Brown.

"Where Did Our Love Go," I felt that we must surely be due something for this accomplishment.

Mrs. Edwards was the chief executive of International Talent Management Inc. (ITMI), who booked and managed us, and she was also Mr. Gordy's sister. When I went to see her and asked about the money that must be owed to us after our recent success, I was utterly shocked to hear her reply, "There is no money. Motown, who manages you, books you, and handles the public relations, etc., managed to get you on the Dick Clark tour only because he wanted Brenda Holloway. I told him to take you, too, and they hesitantly agreed."

"But, Mrs. Edwards," I replied, "we've been on the road for three months, and most of the shows were sold out. Surely, there must be some money coming to us."Looking me squarely in the eyes she said, "You were only paid $600 a week, dear. Deduct from that the price of room and board and food for yourselves and Mrs. Ross, and that leaves nothing." Wow! You could have knocked me down with a feather boa. I was absolutely crushed to hear this.

She then proceeded to explain to me that what we needed to concentrate on was not the paycheck at the end of the rainbow, but the quality of our stage show. According to her, audiences would come to see us perform, and if they were happy with what they saw and heard, then they would buy more and more of our records, and attend more of our shows, then the money would come. I could see from this little encounter that, for The Supremes, the work had just begun.

Although we did not get the huge paychecks we expected, what we received instead was a series of valuable lessons in "show business." Although I didn't go to college at this time, I was about to receive a full education on how to become a star, and how the entire music business worked. It was like the three of us were graduating from Motown University, Class of 1964!

I am frequently asked about how the artist development department started at Motown. It was made up of many professional people. One of them was Thomas "Beans" Bowles, a musician, who first put the idea of the department to Mr. Gordy. He had come back from one of the earlier "Motortown Revue" tours and told Mr. Gordy, "That tour was great, but these kids need some help. Their singing was good, but walking on and off stage chewing gum and dragging their feet was horrible." Mr. Gordy took his advice seriously. He fully understood that it was far more important to create classy acts than it was to only produce hit records. And that was probably the beginning of Motown's artist development department.

Motown often gets the credit for polishing up our act, and Cholly Atkins and our beloved Mrs. Powell were certainly very influential. For our stage acts, Motown chose Cholly as our choreographer. He was a well-known dancer in the duo Coles and Atkins from the vaudeville days, and he came up with many of the stage moves that made us famous.

There was also Maurice King, who had been a big band leader at the Flame Show Bar in Detroit, where most of the top black entertainers appeared, such as Nat King Cole, Ella Fitzgerald, and Della Reese. And there was Harvey Fuqua, of the group Harvey & The Moonglows, too. Both our image and our stage act were shaped by Maurice. For example, he is the one who wrote such beautiful words for Diane to deliver in the middle of our rendition of "Somewhere," and wrote the comic banter that Flo and I were given as part of our nightclub act.

Mrs. Maxine Powell, in particular, was a known commodity in Detroit. A successful model with a reputation for poise and beauty, she set about giving us lessons in the proper way to act, look, and conduct ourselves in every situation. She would say to us, "One day you will be singing for kings and queens." According to her, "All of you are diamonds in the rough; we are here just to polish you." And polish she did!

Not only did The Supremes receive this star treatment, but our fellow Motown acts, including Martha & The Vandellas and even the guys—The Temptations, The Four Tops, and Marvin Gaye—were also "students" at this exclusive in-house finishing school. We were all taught how to command respect wherever we went.

Fortunately for us, Berry Gordy and Motown had their eyes on a much bigger prize than radio and pop stardom. It was their intention to turn their new singing stars into proper ladies and gentlemen, who were perceived as "first-class acts." They wanted to make certain that we could not only appeal to record-buying teenagers, but also to a wider audience.

Actually, I feel we surpassed anything that they thought could happen. Yes, we were hoping for hit recordings, but in 1965, when we scored five consecutive No. 1s, it was a first. It was unheard of at that time.

Meeting royalty all over the world, mixing with "café society," and ultimately becoming friends with princes and princesses: we did all that and more. Wow! So, when you look back, maybe everything was meant to be: Flo picking the name "The Supremes," Mrs. Powell telling us that one day we would sing for kings and queens—these dreams all came true! All of our dreams were becoming a reality, yes, but does money make you happy? We were about to find out.

Meanwhile, we were developing an international reputation. We had our first No. 1 song in the U.K. with "Baby Love" (1964). There was a demand for us in every country. We even recorded "Baby Love" in German. Since we didn't speak German, we recorded it phonetically. "Baby Love" was also a big hit in the Netherlands and Norway. The next thing we knew, we were touring all across Europe. We were not only at No. 1 in the U.S.A., we were suddenly Top 5 in Europe and Top 20 in Australia.

The songs and the appealing image of The Supremes also seemed to play a role in the Civil Rights movement. We were three young black girls whom the whole world admired. This was unprecedented! The U.S.A. was changing at that time, and we were riding the crest of that change with our hits. Martin Luther King was speaking about "love," and so were we. Almost instantly, we were welcomed into the living rooms of millions of people here in America, whether they were black or white, or whatever nationality.

This was not something that we created on our own. There had been many black stars before us whose shoulders we stood on: Sammy Davis Jr., Sidney Poitier, Lena Horne, Ethel Waters, Josephine Baker, Dorothy Dandridge, and Diahann Carroll, to name just a very few. Such stars were not even allowed to stay in the same hotels whose nightclubs they headlined, because they were black.

The 1960s, the Motown Sound, and "Where Did Our Love Go" went hand in hand with people standing up for their rights. We were glamorous, and we sang about love. We became the three black faces on *The Ed Sullivan Show* every Sunday night. Diahann Carroll was another black face on television. My favorite actor, who was a huge movie star at the time, was Sidney Poitier. Things were changing. Black people were being seen differently now.

The Motown Sound helped open up the borders of the world. We were so thankful to Motown and Berry Gordy for believing in us and sticking with us until we found the right sound, and to Holland-Dozier-Holland for writing the right songs for us to break through all the way to the top of the charts. Because of the huge success of "Where Did Our Love Go" and "Baby Love", there was a mad dash at Motown to follow up the songs with more hits. It wasn't long before we scored our third, fourth, and fifth No. 1 international hits in a row: "Come See About Me" (1964), "Stop! In The Name of Love" (1965), and "Back In My Arms Again" (1965). Our dreams were coming true right in front of our eyes. With every chart topper, we moved higher up the totem pole at Motown.

We started to do bigger shows in the U.S.A. at this time, working with many of the stars of the day. One of the first places we went to outside of the States was Bermuda. We were there for two or three weeks.

On September 12 to 21, 1964, we were one of the headlining acts at the Murray the "K" all-star show at the Brooklyn Fox Theater in New York. This time, we featured alongside Dusty Springfield, The Shangri-Las, Jay & The Americans, Little Anthony & The Imperials, The Ronettes, and Millie Small. Our Motown family was well represented, too, as also on the bill were Marvin Gaye, The Temptations, Martha & The Vandellas, The Contours, and The Miracles.

Soon, the artist development department started upping the game for us on our travels around the world. We would record for two or three hours, then go to work with Cholly Atkins on new choreography. We had watched exactly the same thing happening with Mary Wells before us. Now it was our turn.

Florence, Diane, and I celebrate outside *The Steve Allen Show*, where we performed our No. 1 hit "Where Did Our Love Go" in 1964. Notice the crystal ball necklaces, and how low our heels were. We always wore low heels for dancing—never the stiletto heels that they wear today!

Below and bottom: Photographers capture our arrival at the London headquarters of EMI in 1964. Our British-inspired outfits are accessorized with bowler hats and umbrellas, and are featured on the album cover for *A Bit of Liverpool* (1964). Yes, even back then there were paparazzi following us!

Globe-trotting Supremes

1964 to 1965

Our first trip to the U.K. took place in late 1964. We left Detroit on October 7 to travel to the U.K. for a series of concerts and television performances, to support the success of "Where Did Our Love Go" (1964). On October 8, we visited the offices of EMI Records. EMI was the company that distributed Motown Records in the U.K., and our label over there became known as "Tamla-Motown Records."

That was also the day that Flo, Diane, and I posed outside for the now-famous photographs of us wearing green mod skirts and jackets, and holding very British-looking umbrellas. One of the images from that session appeared on the cover of our fan favorite album *A Bit Of Liverpool* (1964). On that particular album, The Supremes saluted the "British Invasion" by recording songs made popular by The Beatles, Peter & Gordon, Eric Burdon & The Animals, The Dave Clark Five, and Gerry & The Pacemakers. We had such a ball singing all of those tracks. On October 15, at the Ad Lib Club in London, we had our first brief meeting with two of The Beatles: Paul McCartney and Ringo Starr. It was loud in that club, and we had to shout to be heard, so we didn't have an in-depth conversation at all.

Back in the U.S.A., on October 28 and 29, 1964, we appeared in concert as part of the all-star rock 'n' roll show known as the *T.A.M.I. Show*, which stands for Teenage Awards Music International. It was held at the Santa Monica Civic Auditorium. Thanks to our records "Where Did Our Love Go" and "Baby Love" (1964), we were officially one of the top hit-makers in the business! The other headliners on the show were The Rolling Stones and James Brown. Also on the bill were The Beach Boys, Chuck Berry, Marvin Gaye, Lesley Gore, The Miracles, Jan & Dean, Gerry & The Pacemakers, and Billy J. Kramer.

Two nighttime concerts and one afternoon show were filmed and edited together to make a limited-run theatrical film, which became legendary. In fact, Academy Award-winning filmmaker Quentin Tarantino referred to the filmed version of the *T.A.M.I. Show* as: "In the top three of all rock movies."

We sang four of our recent songs, "When The Lovelight Starts Shining In His Eyes" (1963),"Run, Run, Run" (1964), our latest No. 1 hit single "Baby Love," and "Where Did Our Love Go." It was lots of fun being a part of such amazing rock 'n' roll shows, with all of the other hit-makers of the day. Among the longest lasting friendships that came out of this particular show was the one I formed with Bill Wyman of The Rolling Stones. Many years after we first met, Bill asked me to tour as a special guest artist with him and his band The Rhythm Kings in the U.K. In 2014, we then did another tour together all across Europe.

The same week that we performed at the *T.A.M.I. Show*, Motown released our next hit single, "Come See About Me" (1964). Actually, "Come See About Me" was not the first choice, but another female singer by the name of Nella Dodds had heard the song on our album and released it, so Motown decided to rush our version out. We shot straight up the charts to No. 1, thus continuing our winning streak of chart-topping singles. In October 1964, our album *A Bit of Liverpool* was released, and made it to No. 21 on the *Billboard* album charts and No. 5 on the R&B album chart.

During November and December of 1964, we were in and out of the Hitsville studio to record tracks for our forthcoming album, *More Hits By The Supremes* (1965). At the end of the year, we found ourselves so much in demand that we spent the Christmas holidays in New York City. We had our first rehearsal for what was to become our debut appearance on the top-rated US television variety program, *The Ed Sullivan Show*.

I will never forget our first performance on *The Ed Sullivan Show,* on December 27, 1964. The hour-long television program was well known for launching and making singing careers. It was a popular family show. In fact, the whole British Invasion of the musical charts started when The Beatles debuted on Ed's show earlier that year, in February. Now it was our turn. And, what a turn it was! We performed "Come See About Me," and it was a great success. For me, it felt like the best Christmas present possible.

Over the next six years, we were guests on *The Ed Sullivan Show* another fifteen times. Ed was so charming and gracious toward us that after a while it started to feel like it was our own personal television show.

Times were changing, and both The Supremes and The Beatles helped usher them in. Because of segregation in America, black people were only

Opposite top and bottom: Florence, Diane, and I make the most of the sunny weather in Swinging Sixties London. We wear bright pink girlie dresses as we pose for a relaxed series of photographs (1964).

seen on television in subservient roles, such as maids and butlers. Here, we were being treated like stars by Ed Sullivan, so our appearance on the program was quite unique.

Even as 1965 was beginning, it was already destined to be one of our most exciting years yet. It seemed that The Supremes were gaining momentum with every passing day. My life was so exciting, and I loved every minute of it! At the beginning of the year, we were voted the number one female group in *Music Business* magazine, and the number three top group in the U.K.'s rock publication *New Musical Express*.

Whenever we had a free day, we flew into Detroit to record song after song. We were recording Nashville songs for our *The Supremes Sing Country, Western & Pop* album (1965) and ballads for an unreleased album titled *There's A Place For Us*, as well as songs for our album *We Remember Sam Cooke* (1965). This was in addition to our regular contemporary hits albums. So many of the songs we recorded in this era remained unreleased until the CD era of music, when they appeared on special "deluxe expanded" versions of our reissued discs. Eventually, in 2004, *There's A Place For Us* was released in its entirety, which includes my solo on "Our Day Will Come," and Flo's powerful version of the song "People."

These were albums on which you could hear the tight blend of our harmonies, as well as all of us taking turns singing lead vocals. There were some amazing recordings that came from these sessions; Diane was shining on everything at this time. She had really come into her own. The tribute album, *We Remember Sam Cooke*, has one of the finest examples of Florence's lead singing, on the track "Ain't That Good News."

While all of this was going on, our television schedule was incredibly exciting, too. Since we had quickly become Detroit legends, we appeared on *Bill Kennedy's Showtime* and on *Teen Town*, which was hosted by a local D.J. named Robin Seymour. We also made our debuts on the primetime teenage rock show *Hullabaloo*, a classic variety program *The Hollywood Palace*, and a Dick Clark-produced show called *Go-Go*, which was shot in Palm Springs, California. Our fourth consecutive No. 1 hit, "Stop! In The Name Of Love" (1965), was released and instantly shot up the charts. In addition, "Baby Love" was nominated for a GRAMMY Award®.

We flew to London on March 16, 1965. The excitement that was building in the U.S.A. around the British Invasion was about to be paralleled by The Supremes/Motown invasion of the U.K. I will never forget stepping off the airplane in London to be met by cheering crowds of British music fans holding signs and banners to welcome us as show business stars. This was the way America had welcomed The Beatles. The Motown Appreciation Society organized this touching display, spearheaded by Dave Godin. It was one of our first impressions of the British Isles, and it was a truly thrilling one.

As a result, we were all over the British press. One publication even said, "Three black Negresses have landed on the shores of Great Britain." However, we were welcomed in Europe and the U.K., not as black people, but as stars!

Thanks to our hits and the recent success of Martha & The Vandellas, Stevie Wonder, The Miracles, The Temptations, and The Four Tops, we were now part of a growing wave of Motown popularity on the U.K. charts. But it was The Supremes who scored the first No. 1 hit in the U.K. with "Baby Love." It was like America and England had opened their gates, and we were the musical ambassadors for diplomacy.

Our first time at the Apollo Theater, New York, was as part of the Motortown Revue in 1963, in which we wore short dresses and our own hair. This was before we embraced makeup and wigs. I have great memories of that gig. The show, which featured a roster of Motown artists, had already toured America in 1962, but The Supremes had not been included because we did not have any hits at that time. We joined the Motortown Revue U.K. tour in 1965, after we had enjoyed a few small local hits and before we did the Dick Clark "Caravan of Stars" tour.

Thanks to the increased global presence of both American and British music, we were truly at the forefront of a 1960s cultural explosion. It was an exciting time, and The Supremes were right in the middle of it. It was thanks to the Motown machinery of Berry Gordy, Barney Ales, the attorney George Schiffer, and Mrs. Edwards that our U.K. tour took place. They really worked their magic getting Tamla-Motown Records into the international marketplace in the U.K. and Europe.

One of the most exciting things to happen to us on this tour of the U.K. was our appearance on a television special, which turned out to be

Below: We take a break from TV rehearsals while out on tour in New York. In those days we still had chaperones. Diane's mom, Mrs Ross, was one of my favorites and can be seen sitting behind us (left).
Bottom: Waiting at the airport at Heathrow can be a pain even when you are permitted to smoke indoors.

We often had to do interviews while out on the road. I could not decide which hairpiece to put on—the blond hairpiece (below) or the one I eventually ended up wearing (bottom). It seems Diane and I both decided to be brunettes. Flo wore a red flip; she was actually a blondish red head for real. Diane always called Florence "Blondie."

a tribute to everything Motown. One of the biggest rock 'n' roll television programs there at that time was called *Ready, Steady, Go*. As ambassadors of the "Detroit Sound," we were booked to be the stars of an episode titled "The Sound of Motown." And the special hostess of the evening was our friend, British superstar Dusty Springfield. The evolution of the special episode had started when Dusty told her manager, Vicki Wickham, about the fabulous acts on Tamla-Motown. Vicki was not only a huge fan of all the Motown artists, but she was also the assistant producer of *Ready, Steady, Go*. She was one of the people who presented The Supremes to the show's producers and made everything happen.

The BBC's designers created a great stage set-up for us, with pictures of The Supremes, The Vandellas, Stevie Wonder, The Miracles, and The Temptations. We taped "The Sound of Motown" on March 18, and it was to become a wonderful showcase for all of us. After recording the television show, we began our concert tour of the U.K. However, The Temptations returned to the States for a series of gigs and were not part of the Motortown Revue tour in the U.K.

Unfortunately, ticket sales for the "Tamla Motown Show", as it was billed in the U.K., were nowhere near as successful as Motown had hoped. It was not until April 28, after the tour had finished, that the BBC aired the television special. Had the program been shown before the concert tour, the theaters would have been sold out for sure. Georgie Fame, the British singer of the hit "The Ballad of Bonnie & Clyde" (1968), was added to the bill to help ticket sales. Georgie and I have remained friends ever since, and we have both toured with Bill Wyman on and off.

The road tour began on March 20 at the Astoria in Finsbury Park, and the next night it headlined the Hammersmith Odeon in west London. Then we toured throughout England, Scotland, and Wales. We called it "the ghost tour" because of the lack of crowds.

Fortunately for everyone on the tour, the fans who did come to those shows absolutely loved us, and soon the word-of-mouth raves started a groundswell of British, Irish, Scottish, and Welsh popularity. The loyalty of The Supremes' U.K. fans truly continues to this day.

After our month in the U.K., our next stop on the tour was Paris and Olympia Hall. It was so exciting to be in Paris, after touring all over England. Again, it was a "dream come true" moment for real. The show in Paris was a sell-out success, and there were so many people in the audience, including Sarah Vaughan, Marlene Dietrich, and numerous famous French singers I didn't know. The show was also recorded for French television, and as an album. The result, *Motortown Revue Live in Paris* (1965), is a collector's item today.

The French television producer had the idea to film us frolicking about down the middle of Paris's busiest boulevard, the Champs-Elysées, during rush hour. Imagine us doing that on Fifth Avenue in New York City! The car that drove in front of us blasted out our records over the loud speaker. Can you believe it? We all took part gladly until the policemen tried to stop us. Little did we know that the director did not have a license for this little charade. It was fun, though, and after all we were crazy American stars who came to show Paris what we were all about!

When we were back in the U.S.A., Motown released our fifth consecutive No. 1 single, "Back In My Arms Again" (1965). This remains one of our most beloved hits, as Florence and I were actually named as characters in the lyrics. What was so cute and appealing about this song is that Diane, in her lead vocals, asks her closest girlfriends their opinion about the boyfriend troubles she has been experiencing. In the context of the song, she speaks about not trusting her girlfriends' negative opinions of her boyfriend, because "Mary" recently lost her own boyfriend and "Flo" is dating a notorious "Romeo." We have Holland-Dozier-Holland to thank for this wonderfully fun song that turned Florence and I into bona fide rock 'n' roll characters!

In 1965, there developed a need and a demand for the three of us to be always dressed in a chic fashion both on stage and off. Our schedules were such that we would often go from an interview straight to a television show, so we always had to be "dressed up" to the nines. We were fashionably attired, nicely made-up and in full Supremes mode 24/7. Fortunately, we all adored clothes and loved to shop, so this was not a problem at all. Whenever we attended press interviews, we were able to express ourselves in our own personal taste, by wearing more casual clothes and accessories. This was the era of bell-bottomed pantsuits, mini skirts,

Below and bottom: The Motor Town Revue arrives in London, England in 1965. Here we are at the EMI reception where we all posed for the press: The Temptations, Stevie Wonder & The Miracles, Martha & The Vandellas, and The Supremes. Is that a sixth and seventh Temptation? No, it's two of The Funk Brothers! Later, Flo, Diane, and I sing our hits.

Below and opposite: We rehearse and perform as part of the all-star lineup on the BBC television special *The Sound of Motown* (1965). The groundbreaking show introduced Motown music to a mass audience in the U.K., establishing us as household names. If you think you have seen these dresses lately, you probably spotted the look-alike versions of them in the movie *Dreamgirls*. I loved those red pumps!

Below and bottom: Florence, Diane, and me on tour in Paris in 1965. We go sightseeing all over the city and pause for a must-have photograph in front of the Eiffel Tower.

maxi skirts, go-go boots, and all of the fashions that defined the original mid-1960s "look," and I fully embraced it.

In 1965, we were still au naturel: wearing our own hair—sans hairpieces—with very little makeup. But both Diane and Florence started wearing wigs in public, so that it was easy to change their hairstyles at a moment's notice. Finally, I started wearing wigs as well, so that I could change my hair as easily and quickly as we changed clothes. The *T.A.M.I. Show* was one of the last performances I gave with my own hair, and everyone thought it was a hairpiece anyway. We hired a young man named Gregory, who would get our hairpieces ready with new styles whenever we needed them, and also Winnie Brown, our chaperone who traveled with us. In those days, you could bring hat boxes on flights, as many as you could carry, and believe me we had lots of clothes, accessories, toiletries, etc. Today, they certainly would not allow us on the plane! As we became more famous, we had dozens of hairpieces that we traveled with. Of course, they were very elaborate and beautifully made using real human hair, and they were very expensive, too. In the press, we were christened "America's Sweethearts," and we were expected to personify an image of modern glamour in the way we looked and behaved.

More important than our need for fashionable off-stage wear was our growing need for a stage wardrobe trunk. It was big and full of dresses and gowns for stage appearances, television performances, and photo shoots. Whenever we were in New York City—which was often—if there was even a two-hour break between rehearsals and recording, we would run over to Saks Fifth Avenue for a fast-paced shopping spree.

The high-fashion era for The Supremes was truly under way. It was the beginning of us wearing very elaborate gowns in concert and on television. We had always worn dresses or gowns for our performances, but suddenly they became far more glitzy and glittering. Gone were the short girlie dresses that I loved. This was due to the designers who worked on the television shows. They started bringing us sketches of beautiful gowns. Wherever we went, there was a sense of anticipation that preceded our arrival: "What will The Supremes wear next?"

Our trademark look of being identically clad in elaborately sequined, beaded, fringed, and bedazzled gowns was officially born. Florence, Diane, and I loved our new roles as the music world's favorite "fashionistas." However, our "look" was becoming very expensive, and we began to spend lots of money on our outfits, which Motown deducted from our Supremes bank account. Up until that point, we had been very frugal, only spending money on clothing and necessities. Our largest purchases came when the three of us bought homes for our families. The one I purchased cost $35,000, which was a lot of money at the time.

The term that I came up with to describe our unique stature in the world was "BLAPS." It is my acronym for "BLack American Princesses." We were now living a fairy tale existence, and we were made to feel like show business royalty. It was literally a dream come true!

I have to admit, Motown had a desire to get their acts booked into chic nightclubs all over the world, and Berry Gordy saw The Supremes as the best vehicle to open the doors. It was to the point that we were billed not just as The Supremes, but as "Motown's Supremes." It was great to be Motown's girls, but now I see that they took away some of our glory by "owning" us.

Performing in "café society" was next. Playing the Copacabana was to be The Supremes' crowning achievement, and everything about it had to be done "first class." The Copacabana, located at 10 East 60th Street in New York City, opened in 1940, and was known for bringing top-rated mainstream headliners into an intimate nightclub setting. Among the people who headlined there before us were Dean Martin & Jerry Lewis, Harry Belafonte, Danny Thomas, Della Reese, Joe E. Lewis, Sammy Davis Jr., and Sam Cooke. The club was so famous that in 1947 Groucho Marx and Carmen Miranda starred in a film version, also titled *Copacabana*.

The very idea of The Supremes headlining at the Copacabana was both ambitious and brilliant. It was one thing for us to have hit singles at No. 1 and to appeal to teenage record buyers, but for Motown to establish three black girls as a premier nightclub act in 1965 was a coup.

Our engagement there was very important to us, and extra important to the company. We were booked to open on July 29. Knowing that every aspect of the show had to be right, Berry Gordy hired our musical arranger, Gil Askey, to work for the company. When Gil was told about

Below and opposite: With a photographer in tow, we display our individual styles, wearing colorful frills, fringes, and pantsuits, all styled by Mrs. Powell.

Here we are in the makeup room preparing for a stage performance. After our experience on *The Ed Sullivan Show* I almost always put on my own makeup. Yes, that is Mrs. Powell's L'Oréal "Love that Red" lipstick I'm applying.

I loved this swinging seat. In those days there were so few women around–even in the makeup room. It was a man's world. What great hairpieces Diane and I have on. We are both having them styled.

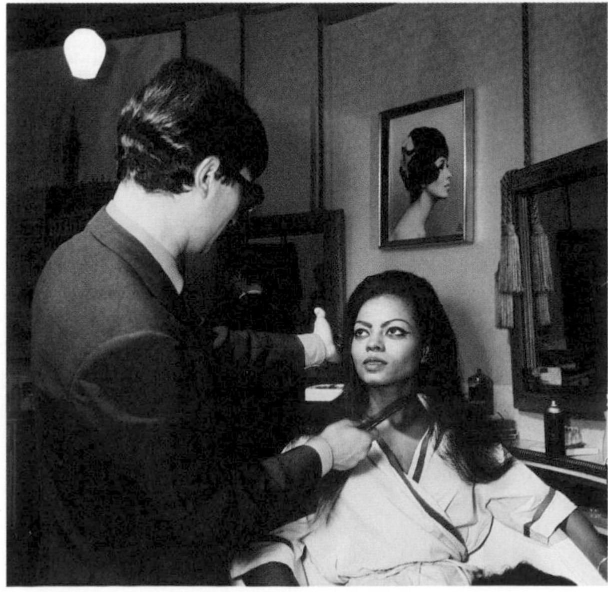

Below and bottom: These shots were taken to promote our debut appearance at the Copacabana in July 1965. At the tender age of twenty-one, we knew we had truly arrived!

our forthcoming Copa engagement, he went to Berry and outlined the entire show he had in mind for us. It was to be a mixture of songs from the American songbook such as Cole Porter, a medley of our Sam Cooke tribute tunes, all five of our No. 1 records to date, and current Broadway tunes from shows, including *Bye Bye Birdie*, *Funny Girl*, and *West Side Story*.

Like most of the other acts who had worked in Motown's artist development department, we knew that this opportunity was different. We had an enormous goal facing us, and it was to be our greatest step yet. Every department of Motown/ Hitsville was involved. The sales department and especially the public relations department, headed by Al Abrams, worked frantically to advertise this event.

For Berry Gordy, this was another very special and exciting achievement: to have his stars —The Supremes—booked at the Copacabana.

Naturally, it was an absolute "must" that our performance was also recorded for an album release. All three of us worked very hard with our new artist development team. Diane worked her butt off at her role, and Flo and I had to synchronize our every finger move to make it look as if they came from the same hand, as if it were the most natural thing in the world. Precision was the name of the game! For The Supremes, it was to be our gigantic trajectory into the big time.

We began rehearsals for the show immediately. The team included musical arranger Johnny Allen. We were coached by Broadway choreographer Cholly Atkins, and of course Mrs. Powell also made certain that everything we did was graceful, classy, and ladylike. As always, Cholly polished our act until it was very tight.

However, it was at this point that problems started to appear in the group. Previously, Florence's big shining moment in our live act had been singing the lead on the song "People." So when it was suggested that Diane might sing lead vocals on "People" instead, it hurt Flo deeply. No particular explanation was given, but it was clear that Diane's star was rising. This marked the beginning of Flo's unhappiness showing through.

As the stage at the Copacabana was quite small, we had to make certain that our every move was performed in such a way that we did not get tangled in the microphone cords. Diane worked separately for hours learning all of the songs. Then she joined me and Flo for the group choreography. Flo and I worked hard to make our synchronized moves look like it was the easiest thing in the world. But believe me it was not. There was one bit of very intricate choreography for the song "Rock-A-Bye Your Baby With A Dixie Melody." We wore straw boater hats for this number, and we each had canes, too. One of the moves involved performing a trick, in which we had to twirl the hats around and not drop them. Once I get a routine or piece of choreography, I have it. Florence was more methodical, but it wasn't long before she too had the routine down. Diane was more deliberate, but once she learned the choreography, she never stopped doing it wherever we were. It took us four months to rehearse the whole show prior to the Copa dates. Eventually, we all had the act perfected.

Berry's youngest sister, Gwen Gordy Fuqua, had a designer friend who had some great ideas for our gowns for the evening. We were shown preliminary sketches, and they looked very fashionable for 1965. Aside from our songs, the most important question concerning our show at the Copa was, "What will we wear?" At this time, we had not started performing in the fabulous gowns that we would become known for.

Backstage at the Copacabana on opening night was bedlam. Fortunately for me, I have always had the ability to remain calm when things go awry. I earned the nickname "cool Mary." But show time was approaching, and we still had not seen the gowns, let alone tried them on to see how they fitted.

"Our new dresses are not here!" Diane announced. Florence, who always had a dry sense of humor in situations like this, said, in her flat comical way, "Well, some of our old dresses are here. But, I know these aren't the ones we're going to wear tonight honey!"

Calmly, I added, "I know they'll be here soon." I often found myself in the role of the "peace maker," even though I did not see myself that way. I guess growing up in a chaotic household as a child had taught me how to keep the peace.

Fortunately, the gowns arrived just in time. We had Maye—Cholly Atkins's wife—helping us out until Mrs. Powell arrived. Once Mrs. Powell got there, she had everything under control, and she quickly unwrapped the dresses. They were blue satin with half sleeves, and around the neckline were flower appliqués that were made of feathers. Since we only had a few minutes until curtain time, we slipped into them, got prepared for the show, and hit the stage.

It was to be a big splash of a night for The Supremes, and Florence, Diane, and I were very excited. The Copacabana was an adult club, and we had all only just turned twenty-one, so for me—and I am sure both Flo and Diane felt the same—our dream had come true. We were the first 1960s pop group to ever play the world famous Copacabana, and everything had to be just right.

The crowd that night included the who's who of the show business world. Famed gossip columnist Earl Wilson was in the audience, and after that night, he became one of our longest and most devoted press supporters, both of The Supremes and of me personally. Comedian Marty Allen and actor Jack Cassidy were there, too, as were some very important disc jockeys, including Murray the "K" and Frankie Crocker. But we were most excited to learn that Sammy Davis Jr. was in the club, and he had brought a whole entourage to witness our splashy Copa debut. I loved that man; he was always so much fun and he was very good to us.

Aside from the songs that we sang, there were several routines and bits of speaking that were just priceless. Most of our dialogue was written by our favorite guy, Maurice King, from the Flame Show Bar.

When Diane introduced us on stage, she said: "Florence Ballard, she's the quiet one...Mary Wilson, she's the sexy one...and me, I'm the intelligent one." The audience loved it. But Flo always made the audience laugh with her reply, "That's what you think honey!" In reality, I thought I was the quiet one, and Florence was the funny one.

One of the songs we sang was "You're Nobody 'Til Somebody Loves You," a popular song written in 1944. One of the lyrics claims that "gold" will not buy you happiness. During the act, there was a pause, and Florence spoke up and proclaimed, "Wait a minute honey, I don't know about all that!" Again the crowd loved it. In fact, the crowd always loved Flo. She spoke her mind, and her comic timing was perfect. For me, Flo was like the great Pearl Bailey, with her snappy off-the-cuff comments. People who only know us from our records never really knew Flo.

The one "glitch" on opening night was the gowns. Although they looked great initially, once we got out on stage, the blue dresses with the huge flowers appeared gaudy, and when we performed our choreography, they were disastrous! The feathers constantly poked and tickled us during the show. To this day, I do not like fake flowers. When we got back to the dressing room, still wearing the dresses with the feather flowers, we all immediately complained.

Gwen understood our frustration and suggested, "Maybe the flowers should come off?"

Never one to hide her feelings, Florence emphatically announced, "Do something!" She then turned to me and said, "Honey, these dresses are a mess, aren't they?" I had to agree. We tore the faux flowers off the dresses, and only wore them once again—without the flowers—for a photo session from which one image was used for the cover of the *Merry Christmas* album (1965). They colorized the dresses red but they're the same dresses. I still wonder where they are, probably in storage at Motown. They might even show up at the Motown Museum.

Feathered dresses aside, the show was a roaring success in every way. We made a huge splash in the press, and the album that we recorded was wonderful. In 2012, a deluxe version of *The Supremes At The Copa* (1965) was released, with us wearing the dresses with the fake flowers on the cover. They do look good in the photographs! One disc includes an unedited version of the show from beginning to end. It remains one of our biggest accomplishments.

From the very beginning, Sammy Davis Jr. was one of our most devoted fans. When Berry asked Sammy to write the liner notes for the album, he gladly and enthusiastically obliged.

While all of this was going on, our next album, *More Hits By The Supremes* (1965) was released and instantly became a Top 10 hit. Looking back, in the span of less than a year we had scored five No. 1 hits and become the biggest-selling and most famous female singing group in the world. Now that we had conquered the sophisticated jet-set world of the Copacabana, we had officially arrived. We were established as a show business commodity, and our jet-setting around the world from this point forward became more hectic, more demanding, and more exciting.

However, this new fast-paced life did not agree with Flo. She was unhappy and moody and I could feel tension mounting. Although both Diane and I loved "the show business life," I think

Below and bottom: We delight the opening night audience at the Copacabana with intricate choreography to accompany our hits. The feather flowers that adorn our gowns are really uncomfortable to wear and are removed for our later performances.

We pose for a photo shoot in a rooftop parking lot in Detroit in 1966. The city loves us because we are the home town girls who made good.

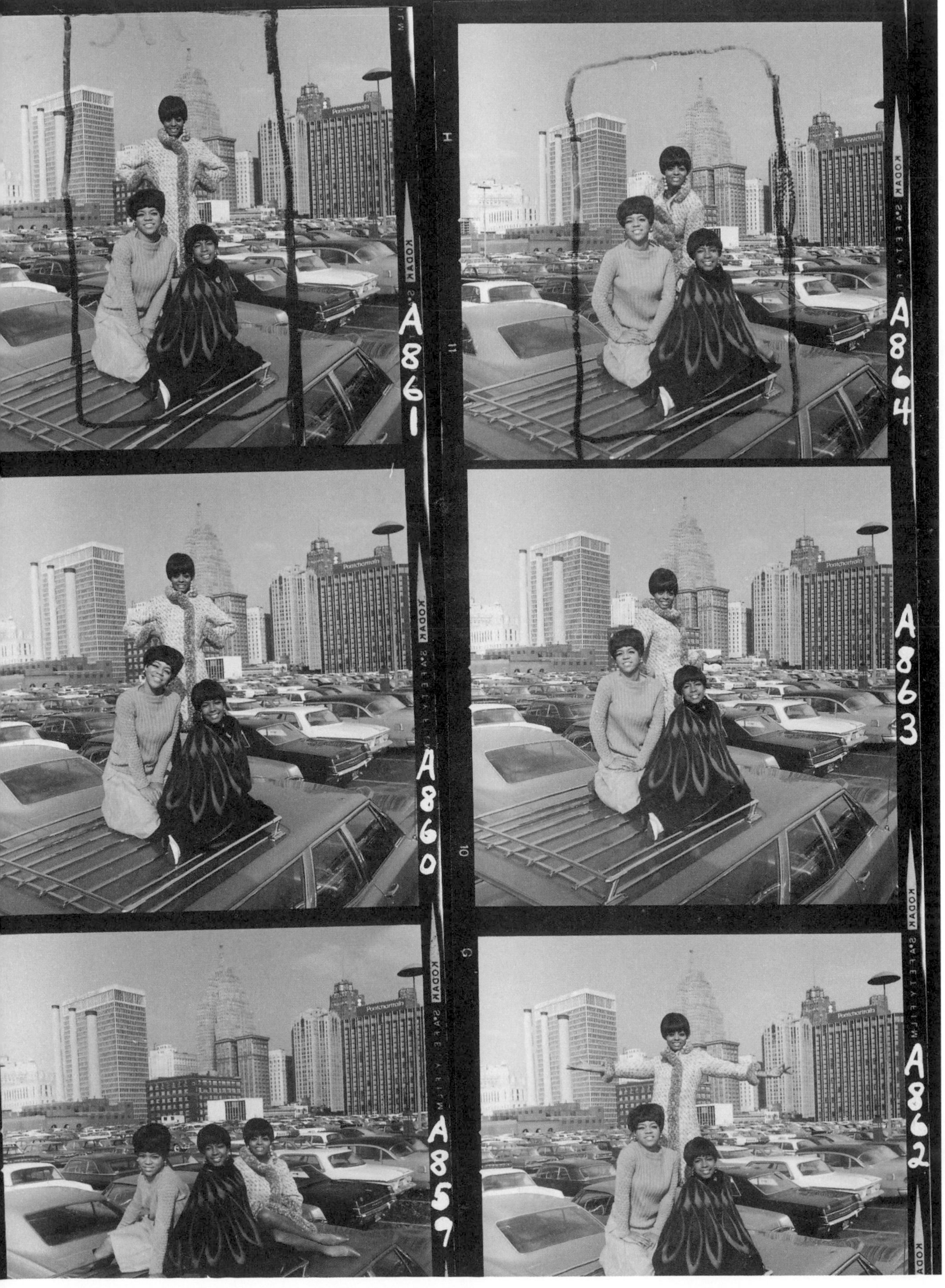
A861
A864
A860
A863
A859
A862
KODAK

Below and bottom: Florence, Diane, and I perform on a television show in 1965 in Detroit. We start by wearing the famous red "shimmy" gowns, with fitted beaded tops and layers of fringing.

Below and bottom: Later in the show we change into straight, ankle-length blue gowns with black lace tops.

Below and opposite: These images are from the filming for *It's What's Happening, Baby*, a television special hosted by Murray the "K" that aired on June 28, 1965. Mrs. Powell, from Motown's artist development department (opposite top), who traveled the world with The Supremes as one of our chaperones, adds a finishing touch to Flo.

It's What's Happening, Baby featured performances by many of the popular artists of the day, interspersed with Murray the "K" urging the youth of America to pursue education and summer employment. We performed "Stop! In The Name Of Love."

the pressure sometimes unnerved even Diane, as she often lost her voice on the road. I, however, adored the life I was now living. After our three-week engagement at the Copa, everyone knew who The Supremes were. "The Primettes" who?

Appearing at the Copacabana became an annual gig for The Supremes. We always loved playing there. Every single night, someone famous was in the audience. Although the Copa was a great nightclub to perform in, the amenities were the worst. You would have thought that there would be a nice large dressing room, but it was very small and situated upstairs in the next hotel. In addition, we had to go through the kitchen in order to enter the stage—and not because we were black. However, we did not mind, because we were headlining a very famous club!

The Copacabana was opened in the 1940s by an Englishman named Monte Proser. However, I am told that Mr. Jules Podell was put in charge of the club by the mob boss Frank Costello. One evening during our gig, we were informed that someone had been found dead on the steps outside the night before. We didn't want to know any details! Mr. Podell would always wear a huge ring on one of his fingers, and when he wanted someone he would bang on the table with that ring. He was a tough guy, but always very friendly toward us; in fact, he too called us "the girls."

What a huge success we had there. In fact, it provided the catalyst for several other nightclubs wanting to book us. In 1965 alone, we also played the Latin Quarter in Philadelphia, Pennsylvania, and the Pompeii Room at the Eden Roc Hotel in Miami, Florida.

In addition to our new nightclub act, we continued to play many other gigs for our teenage record-buying fans. In 1965, we performed at the Michigan State Fair in Detroit from August 17 to September 9, the John F. Kennedy Stadium in Philadelphia, the Oklahoma State Fair, and Lincoln Center in New York City. The last venue is one of the greatest rooms to play, and we appeared in some beautiful yellow chiffon Loretta Young-like flowing gowns at our opening night there. We were on the bill with one of my favorite groups, The Spinners, and the tickets went for $3.50 up to $5.50! The posters from our Lincoln Center gig were created by the famed artist Eula and are now collector's items.

To keep our young fans happy and excited about our performances, we appeared on the national pop music television show *Hullabaloo* a record number of five times in 1965. We were on one episode with our heroes Sammy Davis Jr., Sonny & Cher, and The Lovin' Spoonful. In addition, we appeared on numerous other television shows: *The Ed Sullivan Show*, *The Jackie Gleason Show* with Al Hirt, *The Steve Allen Show*, *The Dean Martin Show*, and *The Tonight Show*. Like the song we were to record, "There's No Stopping Us Now" (1967), our popularity and fame were growing by the minute.

Our hometown of Detroit, Motor City, always kept us in its newspapers. We were local girls who had made it big. Now, we did not simply go downtown and look at all of the beautiful clothes in Hudson's department store—where Diane used to work—but we bought whatever we wanted. Sak's Fifth Avenue was my favorite high-end shop, and we purchased some of our earlier gowns there. Many stores at this time stayed open late for us as we shopped. It was funny, because when we were poor some of them would not even wait on us because we were black; in fact, the sales assistants used to follow us around. It was creepy how they made you feel. Well, the tables had turned now!

In addition to the television programs, we appeared as guest stars on a summer CBS special called *It's What's Happening Baby*, along with Johnny Mathis, The Temptations, The Miracles, Martha & The Vandellas, and Marvin Gaye. We recorded the song "Things Are Changing" (1965), which was produced by the legendary Wall of Sound man, Phil Spector. It was a beautiful song about opportunities in America, and you can really hear Florence in full bloom. She brought such soul to our recordings, and especially to this one.

In 1965, there were hardly any black faces on the covers of magazines, and black people would appear in collages with other people. Nowadays, black faces are featured on every front cover. In 1965, *Ebony* magazine put us on its cover in my favorite red velvet gowns. We were also featured on the front covers of *Time* magazine and *Look* magazine. The Supremes were now "cover girls." This was something that really put us ahead of mainstream America.

Next, we headed off to Europe. We started in Brussels, Belgium, on this trip. On October 2, 1965, we went to Amsterdam for the Grand Gala

These personal images show us enjoying a day out at Disneyland, California. In 1967, we began recording *The Supremes Sing Disney Classics*, but the album was never released.

Below and bottom: Here we rehearse for the upcoming Copacabana show in Studio A at Hitsville in 1965, with Berry Gordy in attendance (below left). We always had fun working in the studio with the artist development team and the musicians.

Below: Harvey Fuqua shows us the exact hand placement to look suggestive. When we learned the choreography, every gesture had to be perfect and it took hours to have the movements worked out so that they looked natural.
Bottom: The Funk Brothers listen on as we perfect our vocals.

Below: Florence takes a rare moment center stage as we break from a photo shoot in Detroit to hang out in an open-top car—still in our gowns, of course! Bottom: This relaxed shot of the three of us was taken in 1965. A photo from this session would be used on the *I Hear A Symphony* album (1966).

du Disque festival. We had been doing so much P.R. on television shows that we were exhausted. So, one evening in our hotel, we decided that we would order food from room service as opposed to going out. We were still in the very early stages of being stars, and there was so much about life, and food, that we did not know. For us, "staying in" was a luxury we rarely had, so that night we decided to stay in just like we did when we were the "no hit Supremes!"

When Diane placed her order, she said, "Chateaubriand: Well done."

"I'll have the same," I said. Not knowing how to pronounce the word.

Looking at the menu, Flo said unsuspectingly, "I'll have this steak—tartare?"

I wondered why the waiter didn't ask her how she wanted it cooked, but then I dismissed it, figuring that he knew what he was doing.

When the waiter came back to our suite with our cart of food, we were really impressed. As he prepared Flo's order, he placed on the plate a mound of raw meat, some chopped vegetables, a sea of spices, and a raw egg. He put on quite an elaborate presentation, creating the "steak tartare" before our very eyes. I began to wonder if I should change my order because it all looked so good. Both Diane and I were looking at Flo, as obviously she had made a great choice.

However, when the waiter presented Flo with the beautiful mound of raw meat, with a bird's nest hollow in the center, and the raw egg in the middle of it, she didn't know what to think.

"What's this?" Flo asked.

"Your steak tartare, ma'am," he replied.

"You don't expect me to eat it like that!" Florence said.

"Well, madame, that is steak tartare."

Not missing a beat, Flo exclaimed, "Honey, you better take this stuff back and cook it!"

I never laughed so hard, and Diane did the same. When the waiter returned with the same concoction—cooked this time—Flo looked at the food and then back to the waiter, and declared, "That's better!" She had a way of saying things that would make you instantly love her.

From there, we went on to London, where we recorded performances on two of the U.K.'s most popular music shows: *Top of the Pops* and *Ready, Steady, Go*. Our next stop was New York City, where we appeared at Sybil Burton's "very, very in" nightclub: Arthur. It was the height of the 1960s "go-go girl" dance craze, and Arthur was the hippest discotheque in town. Talk about The Supremes "a go-go!"

In addition to all this excitement, the album *The Supremes At The Copa* was released in November 1965 and hit No. 11 on the *Billboard* chart, and we also put out our holiday album, *The Supremes: Merry Christmas* (1965). As always, we had recorded more than enough material for two more albums, and the Christmas album was no exception. Two of the best tracks that were laid down at this time were Florence's solo singing on "Silent Night" and "Oh Holy Night." Neither of these tracks were on the 1965 version of our *Merry Christmas* album, but they have since appeared on subsequent reissues. Many people wonder why I talk so much about Flo's talent; possibly it is because very few people know how gifted she was. Because Flo died at such a young age, I feel I have to tell people what I know about her and her talent. I loved both Diane and Flo equally, but Flo can't speak for herself. "Silent Night" and "Oh Holy Night" on our extended *Merry Christmas* album say it all.

We continued to record every time we could; at Motown, recording was expected to continue uninterrupted. When the company released our next single, "Nothing But Heartaches," in July 1965, everyone was shocked when it only reached No. 11 on the charts.

Berry Gordy had a fit, and he went to Holland-Dozier-Holland and demanded that this disappointing chart position would never and could never happen again. He told them that every single released by The Supremes had to be a surefire No. 1 hit. They immediately went to work on a song idea called "I Hear A Symphony" (1965). Diane sang the heck out of this song, and when it became our sixth No. 1 hit in October 1965, it restored us to our winning streak.

During this same era, there was a true "guys vs. girls" battle on the record charts between The Beatles and The Supremes. I think it was more of an issue between the producers than the groups. Anyway, my point is that our song "Come See About Me" (1964) knocked The Beatles' "I Feel Fine" (1964) off the No. 1 spot, when it topped the charts for a second time in 1965. Then The Supremes' "Stop! In The Name of Love" (1965) replaced their "Eight Days A Week" (1964)." And then four years later, our "Love Child" (1968) knocked "Hey Jude" (1968) off peak position.

Below and opposite: James Kreigsmann was The Supremes' number one photographer and he created some of our most iconic images, including these two favorites with me and Florence out front (1965). I always loved the frills at the bottom of these gowns.

(Okay, so I was not on that recording, but I did raise it from the cradle!) For the rest of the decade, The Beatles were the number one male group in the world, and The Supremes were the number one female group. It felt wonderful!

Our first official face-to-face meeting with all of The Beatles happened in August 1965. They were in New York City, staying at The Warwick in Midtown, and we were in town to appear on *The Ed Sullivan Show*. When we arrived at their hotel suite, we were conservatively and smartly dressed in dresses, gloves, hats, high heels, and little fur trimmed jackets. We were chic and fashionably attired, and—more importantly—we were obviously proper ladies (according to my English friend).

Apparently, The Beatles had already been visited by The Ronettes, Bob Dylan, and other stars of the day during this trip to New York. If The Beatles expected The Supremes to be frivolous party girls, they were sadly disappointed. In fact, we were a bit in awe of them. Here we were, about to meet our rivals on the record charts! As we entered their suite, we could instantly detect the smell of marijuana, which is something in which proper young ladies would never indulge.

As we were introduced to Paul, George, Ringo, and John, it was awkward from the start. While three of them were at least conversant, John Lennon just sat in the corner and stared at us. They asked us odd questions about the Motown Sound, and what Holland-Dozier-Holland were like to work with.

Although this was supposed to be an exciting meeting, after a few minutes Florence, Diane, and I had had enough of the awkwardness, and we signaled to our publicist that we were ready to leave, in a ladylike manner of course.

Years later, when I became friends with George Harrison, I asked him about that day at The Warwick. He replied, "We expected soulful, hip girls like The Ronettes. We couldn't believe that three black girls from Detroit could be so square!"

On September 29, our debut big-screen film appearance came in the form of the surfer movie *Beach Ball* (1965). We were seen in a beachside club performing songs that we especially recorded for the movie: the theme song "Beach Ball" and "Surfer Boy" (both 1965). Also in the film were The Four Seasons and The Righteous Brothers. In this same era, we recorded the theme song to another 1965 surfer film: *Dr. Goldfoot and the Bikini Machine*.

On November 14, we were among the headliners to star in the USO A Go-Go Benefit, a big charity concert held at Madison Square Garden, New York. Also on the bill were Joan Crawford, Carroll Baker, Sammy Davis Jr., Johnny Carson, and Robert Vaughan. In December, we made two appearances on *Hullabaloo*, and we were also on Dick Clark's *Where The Action Is*.

Now that we had entered the show business mainstream, we were asked to perform at some incredible events, alongside some of the legends of Hollywood. On December 17, we were booked to open the Astrodome in Houston, Texas, and we starred on the bill with the one and only Judy Garland! This was another highlight of my life that I will never forget.

As a kid, every child in the U.S.A. would sit in front of the television screen for the annual viewing of *The Wizard of Oz* (1939), starring Judy as Dorothy. Judy had, of course, grown up to be one of the most accomplished and famous musical comedy movie stars of all time. We couldn't wait to meet her. Whenever we asked anyone when we could see her, we were repeatedly told, "Later."

After hanging around consistently to get a glimpse of Judy, at long last she stuck her head out of her dressing room door and said to us, "How are you? It's nice to be on the show with you." Then she disappeared back into her dressing room. It was only a brief encounter, but Judy appeared a bit sad. It was sort of disappointing. However, on stage the audience did not see what we had seen, and she was brilliant. That night after the show, we went to a local nightclub where Glen Campbell was playing. He would often come to see us at the Copa and we also appeared on his television show.

Our next single, "My World Is Empty Without You," was released on December 29. It made it to No. 5 in *Billboard* and *Cashbox*, and No. 10 on the R&B chart. I love singing that song even today.

On December 31, New Year's Eve, we were on a float at the Orange Bowl Parade in Miami, Florida. As a Christmas present that year, Berry had given each of us fur coats. He had a New Year's Eve party at his suite at the Eden Roc Hotel. Aretha Franklin and her husband, Ted White, were there. We ended the year feeling like we were sitting on the top of the world, and we were!

This image by Art Shay, titled "Supremely Tired" (1965), documents an unchecked moment, as we wait pensively backstage in our dressing room.

Below and opposite: On the set of *Hullabaloo* in October 1965. No expense was spared on these iconic outfits. The shoes were dyed the same color as the ankle-length gowns, which were adorned with green and sheer crystals on the bodice and around the hem. The gowns are currently in the collection of the Motown Museum.

The Supremes

Supremes '70

Supremes '70

Supremes '70

Supremes '70

The Supremes Gowns

From the Mary Wilson Collection

Gowns at a glance

"Pristine Supremes" (1964)

"Pink Bow" (1966)

"White de Mink" (1966)

"Multi-Colored Halter" (1967)

"Gun Metal" (1968)

"LaVetta Delight" (1968)

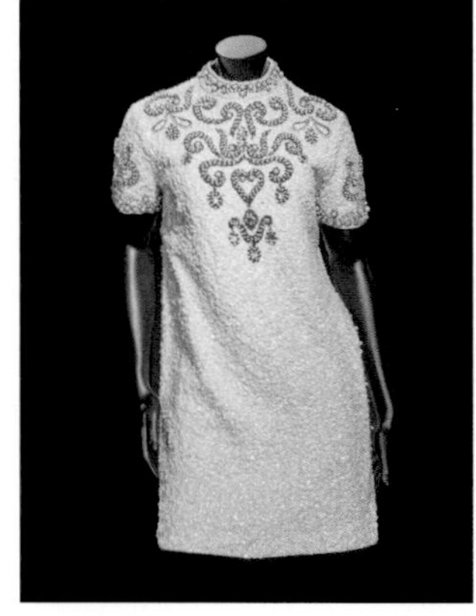
"Goldie" (1968)

"Peach Feathers" (1969)

"Red Hot" (1970)

"Chocolate Feathers" (1971)

"Golden Sunshine" (1971)

"White Rain" (1971)

"Sunburst" (1975)

"Sunburst Cape" (1975)

"Sunburst Opera Coat" (1975)

"Zebra" (1975)

"Green Swirls" (1968)

"Turquoise Freeze" (1968)

"Butterfly" (1968)

"Queen Mother" (1968)

"Orange Freeze" (1969)

"Black Butterfly" (1969)

"Pink Lollipop" (1970)

"Purple Fantasy" (1970)

"Red Twilight" (1971)

"Tropical Lilac" (1972)

"Crème de Menthe" (1974)

"Silhouette" (1974)

"Slinky Sexy" (1975)

"Josephine, Marilyn & Bessie" (1975)

"Blue Icicle" (1976)

"Cranberry Ruffles" (1977)

“Pristine Supremes”

1964

Replicas of the originals

In those days, rock ’n’ roll singers were not really glamorous. We were totally into glamour and we did it all ourselves. We definitely started that trend of glamour, of girl groups getting dressed up.

Material Matte jersey
Embellishments Gathered neck; tied front
Notes These are replicas of the original gowns worn by The Supremes.
Originally worn by Diane, Mary, Florence (1964)
Notable appearances Promotional tour of Germany (1964) to publicize the German language version of “Where Did Our Love Go”

Left Official portrait of The Supremes by James Kreigsmann (1964), mass produced and sent out “signed” to fans.

"Pink Bow"

1966

PAB for Saks Fifth Avenue

Once we arrived at Motown, it was very obvious that they were attracted to our manners and how we carried ourselves. On staff was famed model Mrs. Powell, who further polished our trademark style and grace.

Material Velvet empire-style gown with a central satin bow
Embellishments Beaded trim of silvered glass seed beads; bodice embellished with iridescent piette sequins
Notes These gowns were found and bought on eBay by Tony Daniels, who returned them to Mary.
Originally worn by Diane, Mary, Florence (1966–67)
Additionally worn by Diane, Mary, Cindy (1967)
Notable appearances "Ice Capades" (February 13, 1967, ABC)

Left This group portrait of Diane, Florence, and Mary featured on the Dutch cover for "Reflections" and the Italian cover for "The Happening" (both 1967).

"White de Mink"

1966

Jacobson's of Detroit Department Store

We had loads of faux fur. That was a prestigious kind of way of showing that we had achieved our dreams. We had the money and class to buy what we wanted.

Left Cindy, Mary, and Diane appear at the Deauville Beach Resort in Miami during holiday season in 1967.

Material White shantung silk gown with matching mink trimmed jacket
Embellishments Pearls, seed beads, bugle beads, and blue and crystal rose montees
Notes Coats were worn with another set of gowns at the Hollywood Bowl Show.
Originally worn by Diane, Mary, Florence (1966–67)
Additionally worn by Diane, Mary, Cindy (1967–68)
Notable appearances *The Hollywood Palace* (October 29, 1966, ABC), performed "What Now My Love" with Herb Alpert; *Rodgers & Hart Today* (May 11, 1967, ABC), performed "Mountain Greenery" and "Falling In Love With Love" with Bobby Darin

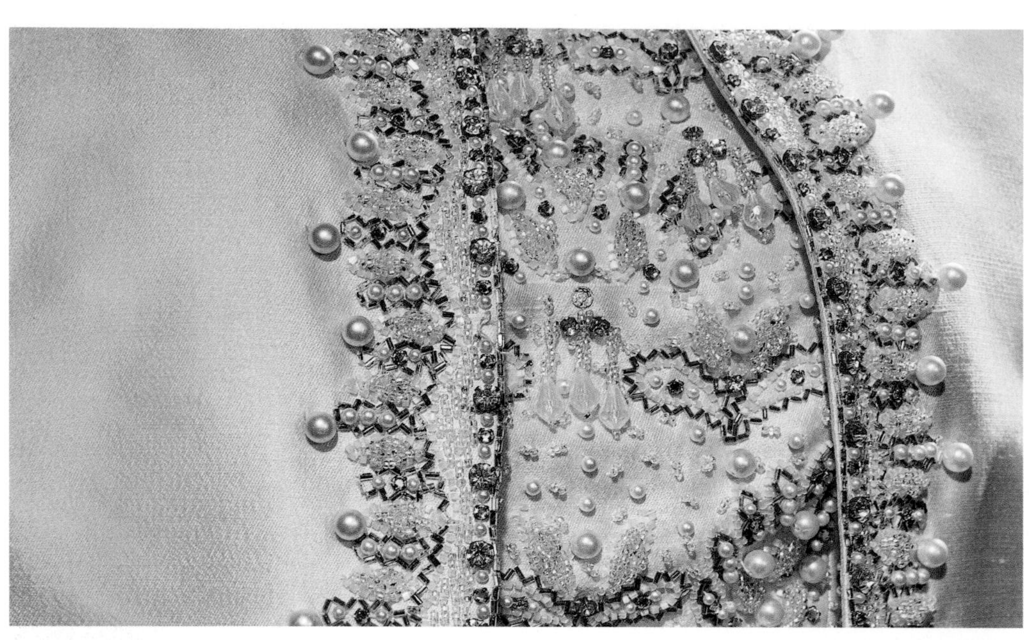

“Multi-Colored Halter”

1967

Designer: Michael Travis

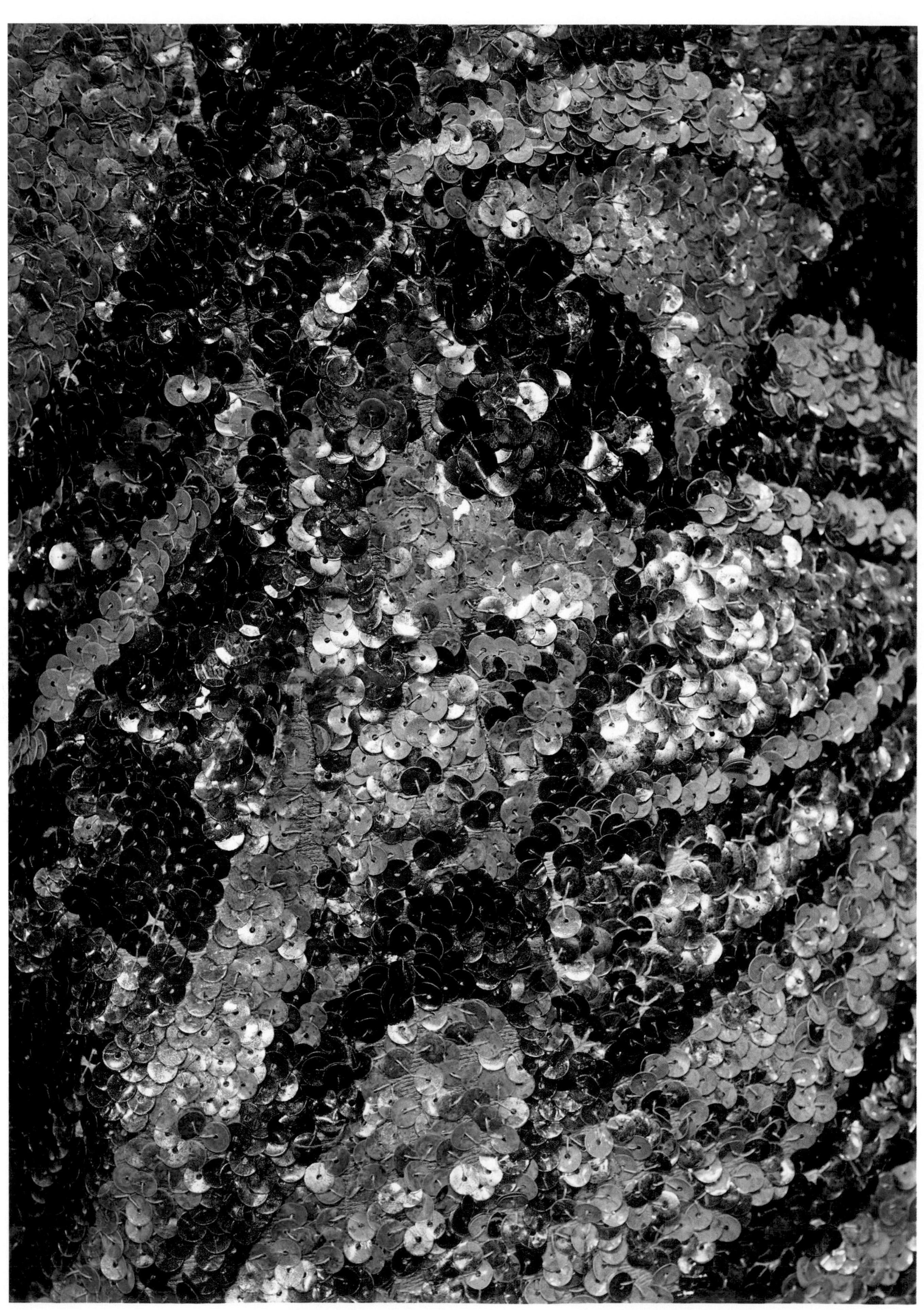

Material Screen-printed and plain chiffon
Embellishments Sequins and glass beads, applied in a "vermicelli" style
Notes The gowns were amended in 1970: additional material was added to the bottom and the leg slits were sewn up.
Originally worn by Diane, Mary, Cindy (1967–69)
Additionally worn by Mary, Cindy, Jean (1970–72); Mary, Jean, Lynda (1972–73); Mary, Cindy, Scherrie (1974–75)
Notable appearances *Tennessee Ernie Ford Special* (December 3, 1967, ABC), performed "The Happening"; *Kate Smith's Remembrance & Rock* (1973), performed "Bad Weather" and "I Guess I'll Miss The Man"; *They Sold A Million* (1973, BBC), performed "Bad Weather"

"Green Swirls"

1968

Designer: Michael Travis

Did Motown mold us into the fashion icons that we were later credited as being? No, they certainly nurtured it and encouraged it, but in reality, when we arrived there, one of the things that impressed them the most about us was our chic look and our strong sense of classy style.

Left Cindy, Diane, and Mary wear the Green Swirls gowns in 1968 for a promotional photo session for the television special *T.C.B.*

Material Screen-printed foulard gown and screen-printed chiffon cape
Embellishments Beaded using various hues of green and citrine beads, with pink bugle beads and crystal rose montees
Notes Altered in 1976. The original neck scarves were removed and beaded shoulder fringes and wrist cuffs were added.

Originally worn by Diane, Mary, Cindy (1968–70)
Additionally worn by Mary, Jean, Lynda (1972–73)
Notable appearances *T.C.B.* (December 9, 1968, NBC), performed "Stop! In The Name Of Love" and "You Keep Me Hangin' On"

“Turquoise Freeze”

1968

Designer: Michael Travis

Material Mushroom pleated silk satin gown, designed to look like a two-piece. The sides of the gown are weighted down by turquoise multi-faceted beads.
Embellishments The elaborate collar, heavily influenced by Hollywood, is beaded with satin and silver bugle beads, crystal rose montees, and white and turquoise seed beads.

Originally worn by Diane, Mary, Cindy (1968)
Notable appearances *The Ed Sullivan Show* (May 5, 1968, CBS), performed a medley of Irving Berlin songs

Opposite Cindy, Diane, and Mary on *The Ed Sullivan Show* in 1968.

"Butterfly"

1968

Designer: Michael Travis

Those Butterfly gown costumes were one of my favorites. We wore them for our final studio album cover, as well as for a television special with The Temptations.... When the arms are stretched wide, the entire cape is just absolutely beautiful.

Left / page 109 Cindy, Diane, and Mary perform at a live performance in 1968.

Material Screen-printed foulard
Embellishments Sequins and rose montees
Notes Featured in promotional material for *T.C.B.* and on the cover of *Cream Of The Crop*.
Originally worn by Diane, Mary, Cindy (1968–70)
Additionally worn by Mary, Cindy, Jean (1970–72); Mary, Jean, Lynda (1972–73); Mary, Cindy, Scherrie (1974–75)
Notable appearances *T.C.B.* (December 9, 1968, NBC), performed "Symphony Medley," "Hits Medley," "I Hear A Symphony," "When The Lovelight Starts Shining Through His Eyes," and "The Impossible Dream" with The Temptations; Festival at Ford's Theatre (December 16, 1970, NBC)

"Queen Mother" 1968

Designer: Michael Travis

Material Silk crepe
Embellishments Diamond-shape pattern outlined in pearls. The center of each diamond contains a large crystal rose montee with smaller rose montees radiating from it.
Notes Each gown weighs around 35 pounds, but does not feel heavy to wear.
Originally worn by Diane, Mary, Cindy (1968–70)
Additionally worn by Mary, Cindy, Jean (1970–71); Mary, Jean, Lynda (1972–73); Mary, Scherrie, Susaye (1976–77)
Notable appearances *Royal Variety Performance* (November 1968, BBC); *T.C.B.* (December 9, 1968, NBC), performed "Somewhere"; *Easter Seals Telethon* (1976), performed "Don't Let My Teardrops Bother You"

"Gun Metal"

1968

Designer: Michael Travis

This is one of those sequin gowns, completely sequined from head to toe. They didn't create the design they just followed the design on the fabric. You can hold [the dress] in one hand—it is very lightweight.

Material Screen-printed chiffon
Embellishment Sequins applied in a tight "vermicelli" style
Notes The original hemline curved up into a side leg slit but was restyled in the early 1970s, with additional material added to close up the split.
Originally worn by Diane, Mary, Cindy (1968–69)
Additionally worn by Mary, Jean, Lynda (1972–73); Mary, Scherrie, Susaye (1976)
Notable appearances *The Ed Sullivan Show* (May 5, 1968, CBS), performed "Always"

Left Cindy, Mary, and Diane perform "I'm The Greatest Star" for the *T.C.B.* special. However, it was cut from the broadcast on December 9, 1968.

"LaVetta Delight"

1968

Designer: LaVetta of Beverly Hills

Material Coats: moiré taffeta; gowns: wool crepe with a sunburst pleated skirt
Embellishments The skirts are decorated with green broken lined bugle beads along the pleating. The halter-neck bodice and coat lapels are beaded with various sizes of emeralds and silver lined seed beads. Rhinestone buttons fasten the coats.

Notes These dresses were the first couture gowns made for The Supremes. The original pea-green beaded V-neck gowns that matched the coats are missing.
Originally worn by Diane, Mary, Cindy (1968–69)
Additionally worn by Mary, Cindy, Scherrie, (1973–74)

“Goldie”

1968

Bought from a store on Hollywood Boulevard

Material Wool
Embellishments Various sizes of pearls, amber-colored glass stones, gold trim, and white sequins

Notes A personal dress belonging to Mary Wilson, who wore it for press conferences and promotional tours.
Originally worn by Mary (1968)

"Peach Feathers"

1969

Designer: Bob Mackie

No matter what the circumstances, The Supremes always looked great. We were always well-dressed, neat, color-coordinated, and fully accessorized. Our image was important to us.

Embellishments Sequins applied in a "chevron" design to the halter-neck, bias-cut gown. A long bugle beaded fringe ties at the back, and a cloud of feathers surrounds the base of the dress.
Notes After Michael Travis left, George Schlatter Productions hired Bob Mackie to design our gowns for our second TV special, *G.I.T.* (*Get It Together on Broadway*).
Originally worn by Diane, Mary, Cindy (1969–70)
Additionally worn by Mary, Cindy, Jean (1970–72); Mary, Jean, Lynda (1972–73)
Notable appearances *G.I.T. on Broadway* (November 12, 1969, NBC), performed "Porgy and Bess Medley"

Left Mary, Diane, and Cindy perform a "Porgy and Bess Medley" on *G.I.T. on Broadway* (1969).

"Orange Freeze"

1969

Designer: Michael Travis

We became the face of the black movement just by being black and prominent—the face of young black women, achieving something.

Left Diane, Cindy, and Mary sing for a live audience on the television variety program *The Hollywood Palace*, October 18, 1969.

Material Silk, lamé, and chiffon blouses
Embellishments Rhinestone buttons decorate the wide cuffs; bugle beads create a herringbone tweed pattern on the trousers
Notes The original jackets were stolen from the Pat Campano/Richard Eckert design studio in San Francisco. Never to be seen again.
Originally worn by Diane, Mary, Cindy (1969–70)
Additionally worn by Mary, Cindy, Jean (1970–72); Mary, Jean, Lynda (1972–73)
Notable appearances *The Hollywood Palace* (October 18, 1969, ABC), performed "Someday We'll Be Together" and "Love Child"; *The Smokey Robinson Show* (December 18, 1970, ABC), performed "Save The Country" and "Friendship Train"

"Black Butterfly"

1969

Designer: Bob Mackie

Material Viscose/rayon velvet; gilt thread
Embellishments Accented with pearls, teardrop fringe, multi-faceted jewels, and glass pearls
Notes Worn for Diane's last performance with The Supremes on January 14, 1970.
Originally worn by Diane, Mary, Cindy (1969–70)
Additionally worn by Mary, Cindy, Jean (1970); Mary, Jean, Lynda (1972–73); Mary, Scherrie, Susaye (1976–77)
Notable appearances *G.I.T. on Broadway* (November 12, 1969, NBC), performed "Opening Medley" with The Temptations; *The Mike Douglas Show* (1976), performed "I'm Gonna Let My Heart Do The Walking" and "Don't Let My Teardrops Bother You"

"Pink Lollipop"

1970

Designer: Michael Travis

Material Four-ply silk and leather
Embellishments Embroidered with metallic silver threads; lattice work on the cuffs and hems; embellished with sequins and stamped metal jewelry
Notes The full three-piece outfits consisted of a bell-bottom jumpsuit, a patchwork vest-style jacket, and a matching low riding hip belt.

Originally worn by Mary, Cindy, Jean (1970–72)
Additionally worn by Mary, Jean, Lynda (1972–73)
Notable appearances *The Glen Campbell Goodtime Hour* (October 18, 1970, CBS), performed "Everybody's Got The Right To Love," "Something," and "Homeward Bound"; *Soul Train* (May 12, 1973), performed "Bad Weather"

Below Original Michael Travis sketch of "Pink Lollipop" gown design (1970).

Opposite Original Michael Travis sketch of "Purple Fantasy" gown design (1970).

Supremes 70

"Purple Fantasy" 1970

Designer: Michael Travis

While the fashion and the music obviously played a huge role in The Supremes' overall impact, it wasn't just about that. My brother would always say, "You girls should be wearing Afros and making a political statement." But I'd always say, "Roosevelt, we are making a political statement. But we're making it our way."

Embellishments Bugle beads, rhinestones, seed beads, calf backing, hanging macro belt
Originally worn by Mary, Cindy, Jean (1970–72)
Additionally worn by Mary, Jean, Lynda (1972–73); Mary, Cindy, Scherrie (1974–75)
Notable appearances *The Flip Wilson Show* (January 7, 1971, NBC), performed "It's Time To Break Down," "Stoned Love," and "We've Only Just Begun"; *Soul Train* (1975), performed "He's My Man"

Left Jean, Cindy, and Mary perform live on stage (1970).

“Red Hot”

1970

Designer: Michael Travis

The grace and confidence that The Supremes personified would inspire a nation and continue to serve as a shining example of modern black womanhood.

Dr. Mark Anthony Neal
Professor of African American Studies
Duke University

Left Jean, Cindy, and Mary sing “If My Friends Could See Me Now” and “Up The Ladder To The Roof” on *The Ed Sullivan Show* (1970). Here, the “Red Hot” gowns have high collars but they proved too warm and were altered to feature a lower neckline in 1976.

Material Plastic-coated threaded fabric
Embellishments Bejeweled and sequinned cummerbund, silver and red sequins, piette sequin fringe, and bell sleeves
Notes First set of gowns to be made for the Mary/Cindy/Jean lineup.
Originally worn by Mary, Cindy, Jean (1970–72)
Additionally worn by Mary, Jean, Lynda (1972–73); Mary, Scherrie, Susaye (1976–77)
Notable appearances *The Ed Sullivan Show* (February 15, 1970, CBS), performed "If My Friends Could See Me Now" and "Up The Ladder To The Roof"; *American Bandstand* (April 17, 1976, ABC), performed "I'm Gonna Let My Heart Do The Walking" and "You're What's Missing In My Life"

"Chocolate Feathers"

1971

Designer: Michael Nicola

The Supremes became role models for a generation. We wanted people to see that black people, or colored people, could be beautiful and successful.

Material Jersey jumpsuits and feathered coats
Embellishments Sequins placed flat, one by one, in the "Norell" style, named after the designer
Notes The jumpsuits have matching feather coats.
Originally worn by Mary, Cindy, Jean (1971–72)
Additionally worn by Mary, Jean, Lynda (1972–73); Mary, Cindy, Scherrie (1973–74)
Notable appearances *The Flip Wilson Show* (1971, NBC); *The Mike Douglas Show* (March 3, 1973), performed "Stoned Love" and "I Guess I'll Miss The Man"; *Top of the Pops* (1973, BBC), performed "Bad Weather"

Left Mary, Jean, and Lynda performing live on stage at the Fairmont Hotel in San Francisco, California, in 1972.

"Golden Sunshine"

1971

Deisgner: Michael Nicola

Those shimmery dresses —for the first time I think people saw women of color looking affluent on television.

André Leon Talley
Former editor-at-large
Vogue

Material Wool
Embellishment Crystal rhinestones run from the neckline to the décolletage, then down the side split and along the hemline
Notes The sleeves were removed in the late 1970s. Mary recalls: "I really liked the sleeves, but they were terribly hot to work in." The wool also had a tendency to snag on the rhinestones.
Originally worn by Mary, Cindy, Jean (1971–72)
Additionally worn by Mary, Jean, Lynda (1972–73)

Left The wool "Golden Sunshine" gowns, seen here on Cindy, Mary, and Jean, may have been a little itchy to wear, but they were highly glamorous both with and without the sleeves.

"White Rain"

1971

Designer: Michael Nicola

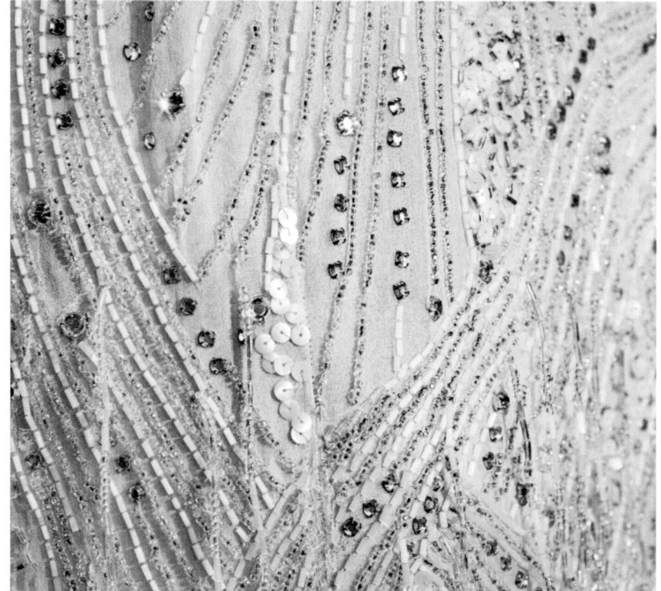

Material White satin
Embellishments Bugle beads, flat white sequins, silver seed beads, and rose montees
Notes Michael Nicola referred to these gowns as "White Rain" in his sketches. Originally, these sequined gowns had sleeves with long beaded fringes, but the sleeves were removed because the beads used to get tangled and fall off. Mary recalls: "Personally, I loved the sleeves with all the beads flying around. They reminded me of shooting stars!"
Originally worn by Mary, Cindy, Jean (1971–72)
Additionally worn by Mary, Jean, Lynda (1972–73); Mary, Scherrie, Susaye (1976–77)
Notable appearances *The Bob Hope Special* (May 12, 1973), performed "Bad Weather"

“Red Twilight” 1971

Designer: Michael Nicola

All the Motown acts were diamonds in the rough, and we at Motown were just there to polish them.

Maxine Powell
Artist development
Motown

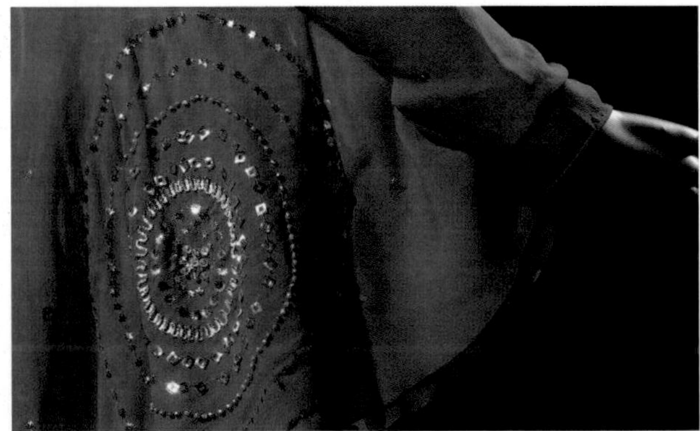

Left The star-shaped gold sequins were sewn on in circles and swirls to embellish the red chiffon with a twinkling effect.

Material Chiffon
Embellishment Star-shaped sequins
Notes The necklines were altered to the V-neck design in 1971. The gowns were worn in their unaltered form in a 1971 photo shoot for the *Touch* album (1971).
Originally worn by Mary, Cindy, Jean (1971)

“Tropical Lilac”

1972

Designer: Michael Nicola

The sky became the limit! Feather boas, capes, dresses with butterfly-like wings, gowns, minis, go-go boots, eyelashes, hairpieces; we wore it all!

Left Lynda, Jean, and Mary wear “Tropical Lilac” live on stage in 1973.

Material Printed jersey
Embellishments Sequins, glass beads, and feathers
Notes These gowns were complimented by removable multi-colored feather jackets. The bra-like bodice was covered with sequins and colored glass beads. They were worn for the front cover image for the *Live in Japan!* album (1973).
Originally worn by Mary, Jean, Lynda (1972–73)
Additionally worn by Mary, Cindy, Scherrie (1973–74)
Notable appearances *The Sonny and Cher Show* (1972, NBC), performed "Your Wonderful Sweet Sweet Love"

“Crème de Menthe”

1974

Designer: Pat Campano/Richard Eckert

Material Chiffon, crepe
Embellishments Sequins, plastic jewels, star rhinestones
Notes Originally, these gowns had plain green chiffon skirts but they appeared washed out in stage lighting so choreographer, Cholly Atkins, had Pat Campano and Richard Eckert add lots of rhinestones. An additional maternity gown was created for Mary.
Originally worn by Mary, Cindy, Scherrie (1974–76)
Additionally worn by Mary, Scherrie, Susaye (1976–77)
Notable appearances *The Merv Griffin Show* (1975), performed "This Dream," "The Way We Were," "Maybe This Time," and "Mercedes Benz"

“Silhouette”

1974

Designer: Pat Campano/Richard Eckert

Material Polyester
Embellishments Sequins and feathers
Notes The original gowns were destroyed in a fire in Mexico in 1974, after which a replacement set was made. An additional maternity gown was created for Mary.

Originally worn by Mary, Cindy, Scherrie (1974–76)
Opposite (L–R) Scherrie Payne, Cindy Birdsong, and Mary Wilson pose for a portrait in 1974 in Los Angeles, California.

"Sunburst"

1975

Designer: Pat Campano/Richard Eckert

Material Silk chiffon with sunburst pleating
Embellishments Nude soufflé seed beads, gold bugle beads, jewels, crystals, and fringing
Notes Two of the gowns (worn by Cindy and Scherrie) had sleeves originally, but they were removed shortly after their creation. The set consists of gowns, capes with internal wire frames, and opera coats.
Originally worn by Mary, Cindy, Scherrie (1975–76)
Additionally worn by Mary, Scherrie, Susaye (1976–77)
Notable appearances *The Tonight Show* (September 23, 1975, NBC), performed "He's My Man"

“Sunburst Cape”

1975

Designer: Pat Campano/Richard Eckert

“Sunburst Opera Coat”

1975

Designers: Pat Campano/Richard Eckert

"Zebra"

1975

Designer: Pat Campano/Richard Eckert

Before The Supremes, the look was smart and simple, like The Shirelles; sassy and sexy like The Ronettes, or tomboyish and provocative like The Shangri-Las. But no one had ever set out to utilize visual signifiers that made them palatable to a white audience.

Howard Kramer
Curatorial director
Rock & Roll Hall of Fame, Cleveland

Left Scherrie, Mary, and Susaye model their "Zebra" stripes. Mary wore the gowns differently throughout her pregnancy. For example, she often wore the kaftan over a black sequined gown. In this photo they wore the kaftans on their own.

Material Cut velvet
Embellishment Black and silver rhinestone banding on dresses and capes
Notes This two-piece set is comprised of a gown that is form-fitting and a kaftan top of the same material. With the kaftan cape over the gown, it appears to be all one piece. Mary also used this kaftan as a maternity top when she was pregnant.
Originally worn by Mary, Cindy, Scherrie (1975–76)
Additionally worn by Mary, Scherrie, Susaye (1976–77)

"Slinky Sexy"
1975

Designer: Geoffrey Holder; Creator: Campert Costume Design, Inc.

Material Velvet
Embellishments Rhinestones and lace
Notes The set consists of gowns, gloves, feathered hats, and fans.
Originally worn by Mary, Cindy, Scherrie (1975–76)
Additionally worn by Mary, Scherrie, Susaye (1976–77)
Notable appearances *The Merv Griffin Show* (1975), performed "Early Morning Love"; *Sammy and Company* (January 3, 1976), performed "He's My Man" and "Early Morning Love"

"Josephine, Marilyn & Bessie"

1975

Designer: Geoffrey Holder; Creator: Campert Costume Design, Inc.

Geoffrey Holder designed a whole dream sequence for our live show, so Cindy Birdsong became Marilyn Monroe, Scherrie Payne became Bessie Smith, and I was Josephine Baker.

Left Cindy, Scherrie, and Mary appeared as Marilyn, Bessie, and Josephine on the front of *Black Stars* magazine, October 1975.

White gown Panne velvet, chiffon, net lace, glass beads, rhinestones
Black/red gown Panne velvet, rhinestones, chiffon lining
Notes Created for the "dream sequence" performed as a live act between 1975 and 1976, in which Mary was Josephine Baker, Scherrie became Bessie Smith, and Cindy (and later Susaye) was Marilyn Monroe. There were multiple accessories such as long gloves, hats, and huge feather fans to match each gown.
Originally worn by Mary, Cindy, Scherrie (1975–76)
Additionally worn by Mary, Scherrie, Susaye (1976)

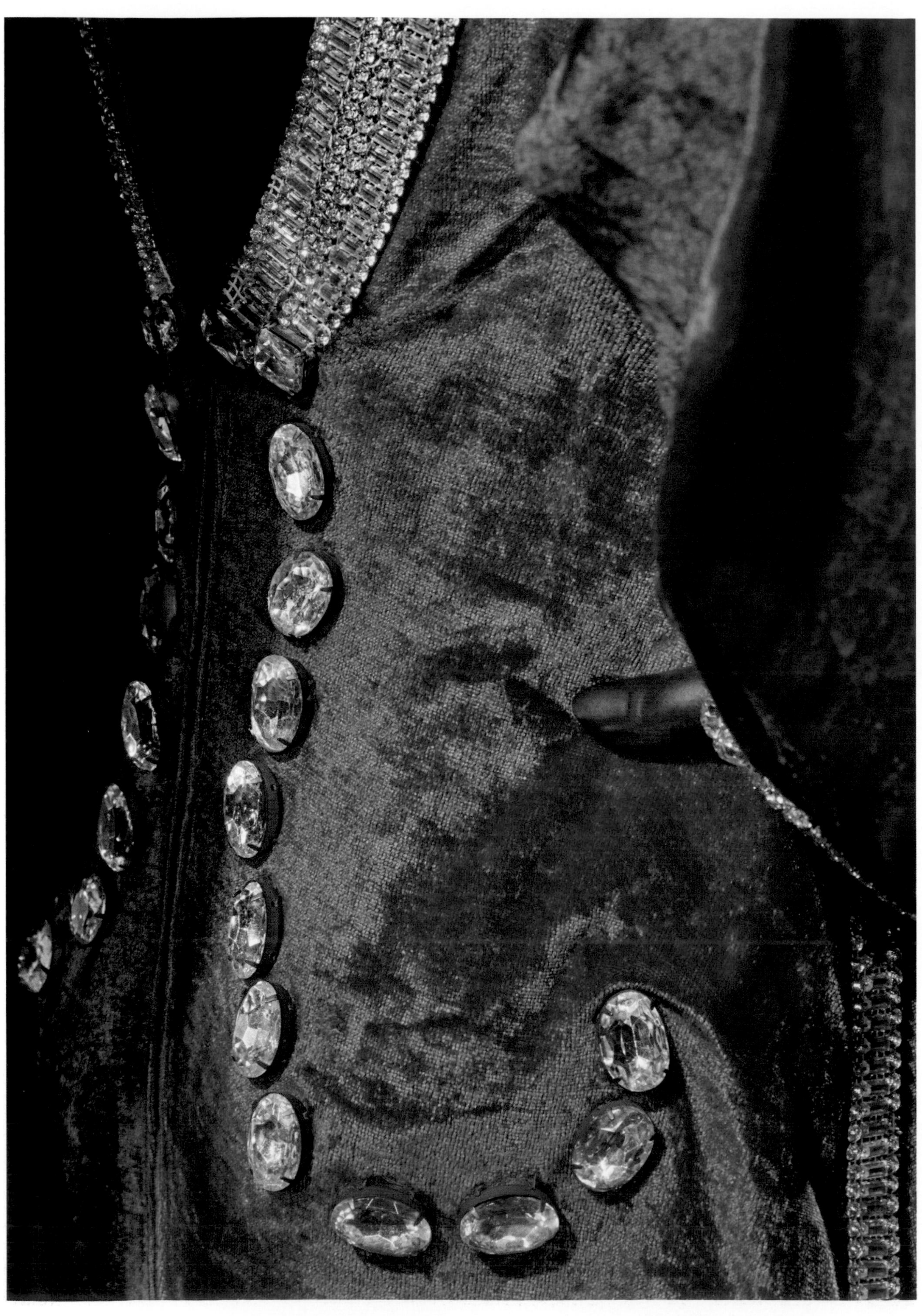

“Blue Icicle”
1976

Designer: Pat Campano/Richard Eckert

Embellishments Brocade bodice with silver trim and short fringing; rows of fabric and clear plastic fringing on skirt
Notes Originally, these gowns were embellished with gold plastic fringing.

Originally worn by Mary, Scherrie, Susaye (1976–77)
Notable appearances *Udo Live '77* (1977), performed "You Are The Heart Of Me" and "Walk Away" with Udo Jürgens

“Cranberry Ruffles”

1977

Designer: Pat Campano/Richard Eckert

Material Chiffon with an embroidered neckline
Embellishments Silver passementerie with rhinestones

Hit-makers to pop legends

1966 to 1977

By 1966, The Supremes were a headline act all over the world. We appeared on magazine covers and endorsed products—there was even a "Supreme" bread. Then in 1967, Flo succumbed to depression, and Cindy joined us. The Supremes stayed in the spotlight, and the hits continued. In 1968, "Love Child" saw the launch of the socially conscious Supremes. Then, after an emotional farewell gig at The Frontier in 1970, Diane went solo. With varying lineups of my choosing, The Supremes continued to record and tour until 1977.

We enjoyed striking dramatic poses in tight-fitting Spandex gold and silver outfits for this 1966 photo shoot. One of the images from the shoot was used on the Spanish 1967 release of "You Keep Me Hangin' On."

The golden years
1966 to 1970

Beginning 1966 with our latest Top 10 single climbing the charts certainly felt good. Everything we touched was seemingly turning to gold. Our busy touring schedule continued at a fast pace. On January 4, 1966, we performed at the Governor's Inaugural Ball at Detroit's Cobo Hall, and on January 15 we were at Arie Crown Theater in Chicago, Illinois. From January 17 to 30, we were back in our hometown, headlining the chic Detroit riverside nightclub Roostertail. Also that month, we were guest stars on television's *The Red Skelton Show*, and we appeared on Robin Seymour's music variety show *Swingin' Time*.

In the January 30, 1966, issue of the *Detroit Free Press*, the headline said: "Success in Eight Easy Lessons: Diana, Mary, and Florence a Year Later...Chauffeurs, the Copa and the Top Hit of '65." All three of us were totally thrilled with what was happening to us. In the article, Flo was quoted as saying, "I just got back from shopping at Hudson's. It was a mad scene. I had to sign autographs—oh, maybe thirty of them—one boy looked up at me surprised, and said, 'Why Florence!' as if to say, 'What are you doing here!'"

In addition to being on stage, this was the part of show business that Flo loved. She so delighted in sharing our success with the fans. But Flo's past trauma, the stress of traveling, and the phoniness of "show biz" were beginning to take their toll on her. This unhappiness was magnified by not singing lead vocals in our act anymore.

That February, we appeared on the television special *Anatomy of Pop: The Music Explosion*. We were filmed singing "My World Is Empty Without You" (1966) in a recording studio surrounded by musicians. We were also the "mystery guests" on the television game show *What's My Line?* In addition, we opened a return engagement at the Copacabana and made our third appearance on *The Ed Sullivan Show*.

On February 18, our ninth album, *I Hear A Symphony* (1966), was released. It made it to No. 8 on the *Billboard* album chart and No. 1 on the R&B album chart. In addition to our hit "My World Is Empty Without You" and the album's title song, we sang the pop standards "Stranger In Paradise" (1953), "Wonderful, Wonderful" (1957), and Rodgers & Hart's "With A Song In My Heart" (1929). This album had Diane standing out front, with Flo and I relegated to singing mainly "oohs" and "ahhs" behind her. The writing was on the wall, and it was obvious that Berry Gordy and Diane were already thinking about her going solo.

By now, The Supremes were a household name across the world. We were on the television and radio, teenagers danced to our music, and their parents came to see us at chic nightclubs. The Supremes also had a perfectly charming image that was ideal for product endorsements. We had already started doing both magazine and radio ads for Coca-Cola in 1965. In March 1966, a local Detroit baker, Schafer Bakeries, came up with the idea of marketing a brand of "Supremes Bread." We were totally up for it! Another endorsement deal was made for us to star in a national television commercial for Arid Extra Dry Deodorant. Honey, we Supremes worked hard, and we were everywhere!

Later that month, we guest starred on *The Sammy Davis Jr. Show*. For this program, we appeared with the group who were once the biggest female trio in recorded history, The Andrews Sisters. What fun we had with them! I had grown up listening to the music of Patty, Maxene, and LaVerne Andrews, and I loved their close harmonies. To have some fun with each group's musical fame, we sang several of their hits, and they sang several of ours. At rehearsals, we somehow naturally paired up and struck up friendships with the girls. On the set, Diane became friendly with Patty, Flo, and Maxene had a lot to talk about, and I hit it off with LaVerne. Among the songs of theirs that we sang were "Bei Mir Bist Du Schoen" (1937), "Roll Out The Barrel" (1939), and "I'll Be With You In Apple Blossom Time" (1941). They, in turn, gave their rendition of "Baby Love" (1964), "Where Did Our Love Go" (1964), and "Stop! In The Name Of Love" (1965).

Throughout the year, we toured constantly, in theaters, auditoriums, and chic nightclubs. My favorite club was Blinstrub's in Boston, which we played from March 22 to April 3. However, the touring began to wear on Florence, and she started to drink more than she had in the past. None of us were big drinkers; we would maybe have a glass of wine with dinner. But Diane and I noticed that Flo had begun to drink more.

On April 3, our next single, "Love Is Like An Itching In My Heart" (1966), was released. Diane is really "kicking it" on this upbeat song, while Flo and I are "jamming" on the background vocals. It made it to No. 9 on the *Billboard* Hot 100 charts,

Below and opposite: We were fitted with beautiful geisha outfits on our tour of the Far East. Berry Gordy documented the trip, shooting us everywhere we went, in Thailand, Manila, and here in Japan (1966).

and No. 7 on the R&B charts. In 2017, when an extended edition of our album *The Supremes A' Go-Go* (1966) was released, it included two fresh "ultimate" mixes of "Love Is Like An Itching In My Heart," which really show off the vocals.

The Dean Martin Show, which we had taped in late 1965, aired while we were in Boston. We performed the song "Mother Dear" (1965) and sang "Love Makes The World Go 'Round" (1958) with Dean and his other guests, Imogene Coca and Jane Morgan. Dean was so very cool and nice. His daughter, Deana Martin, and I are friends now, and we often do gigs together. She is just like her dad, extra nice.

From May 19 to June 8, we headlined the Venetian Room at the Fairmont in San Francisco. Not only was our entire engagement sold out, but we also surpassed a house record that had been set by Nat King Cole. In an article in *Ebony* magazine, titled "The Supremes are Tops," Flo is quoted as saying "They told us that we broke Nat King Cole's mark...Imagine! When I was a little girl, I listened to him all the time. I loved him—the way he sang. You could hear every word. Now, we're breaking Nat Cole's records!"

Playing at the Venetian Room also holds a certain distinction for me. I sang there with every single configuration of The Supremes from 1966 to 1977. It is like a second home!

In June and July 1966, we continued to cut tracks in the recording studio for our forthcoming albums. They included "You Can't Hurry Love" and "Come And Get These Memories" (both 1966) for *The Supremes A' Go-Go* album, and "There's No Stopping Us Now" and "Going Down For The Third Time" (both 1967) for *The Supremes Sing Holland-Dozier-Holland* (1967).

From June 21 to July 3, we headlined at the Music Circus in Lambertville, New Jersey, where Stevie Wonder was one of our opening acts. On June 30, The Supremes appeared on *The Today Show*. It was also Florence's birthday.

On July 13, we were the co-hosts of the Philadelphia-based television program *The Mike Douglas Show*. Also on the bill were our old friends The Temptations. Appearing on Mike's afternoon show was always fun, and it was a great way to reach the housewives and the teenagers as they arrived home from school.

After two hit songs that landed nicely in the Top 10, our latest single, "You Can't Hurry Love" was released on July 25. It flew up the charts and became our seventh No. 1. This song was the one that really returned us to form on the charts. It began our second streak of consecutive back-to-back No. 1 hits: "You Can't Hurry Love" was the first of four chart-toppers in a row. I don't know how I can ever thank Eddie, Lamont, and Brian for all our success. It was their talents—writing and producing The Supremes' sound—that changed our world. Maybe this book is a way of saying "thank you" to Holland-Dozier-Holland, our producers of ten No. 1 records. I love you for giving me my musical life.

"You Can't Hurry Love" not only knocked Donovan's "Sunshine Superman" (1966) off the top spot on the *Billboard* charts, but it also prevented The Beatles' "Yellow Submarine" (1966) from reaching No. 1. This was further evidence that our "guys vs. girls" competition with The Beatles continued, with us the victors again!

Although we did well on the charts against The Beatles, they not only sang their songs, but also wrote them and made a fortune on the songwriting copyright. We might have been winning the battle in the charts, but The Beatles were beating us to the bank! Touché guys!

On August 25, our tenth album, *Supremes A' Go-Go*, was released. It was our first No. 1 album, and it featured our versions of several recent hits, including The Four Tops' "Shake Me, Wake Me (When It's Over)," The Temptations' "Get Ready," Nancy Sinatra's "These Boots Are Made For Walkin'" (all 1966), Marvin Gaye's "Can I Get A Witness" (1963), and the Motown classic "Money" (1959), written by our friend Janie Bradford. As an extra treat, I finally got the chance to sing the lead on my favorite Holland-Dozier-Holland song: "Come And Get These Memories." I really loved that song when I heard Martha Reeves sing it. No one can sing it like Martha. Containing our latest No. 1 hit "You Can't Hurry Love," *Supremes A' Go-Go* was a new high-water mark for us. It also further perpetuated our chart rivalry with The Beatles, as it knocked their album *Revolver* (1966) from the No. 1 spot on *Billboard*'s Top 200 album chart! In fact, it became the first No. 1 album by a female group to ever reach the top spot on that chart in the rock 'n' roll era.

It was such a thrill when we heard that we were going to tour the Far East for the month of September, visiting countries such as Japan, Taiwan, and the Philippines. We had an absolute blast, seeing how different and fascinating life

Below and bottom: We make our first appearance at The Cave, Vancouver, Canada, in 1966. The supper club venue, with its cave-like interior, hosted first-class acts throughout the 1950s, 1960s, and 1970s.

Below and bottom: We appear alongside The Andrews Sisters on *The Sammy Davis Jr. Show* in 1966, and sing a medley of hits by The Andrews Sisters.

was in Asia. I loved the art, architecture, and customs as well as the wonderful people we met there. This was a time when people in Japan were still wearing their traditional garb. To observe them in the downtown Tokyo Ginza was just beautiful, to see all the modern neon and glass structures, set off by a parade of men and women walking by in colorful kimonos.

I also fell in love with the Japanese language and the food. I started eating sushi in 1966. While in Japan, we posed for a photo session dressed in Japanese geisha girl outfits, complete with kimonos and elaborate headdresses. Flo, Diane, and I really had fun striking graceful poses to emulate geishas. The Japanese fans were so enthusiastic, warm, and welcoming. I am proud to say that whenever I go to Japan to tour as a solo artist, they are still as excited and gracious toward me to this day. I send out a special "Domo arigato!" to all of my lifelong Japanese fans!

On September 25, we again appeared on *The Ed Sullivan Show*. This time we sang "You Can't Hurry Love" and a medley of our standards from the *I Hear A Symphony* album. There was no stopping Florence, Diane, and Mary! We were a winning combination, and it felt wonderful to be part of all this excitement.

When we returned home in September 1966, we again headlined at the Roostertail club in Detroit. This time around, two shows from the engagement were recorded for a *The Supremes Live At The Roostertail* album, but for some reason it was cancelled. However, it finally came out on CD in 2012 as part of an expanded edition of *I Hear A Symphony*, and it sounds amazing. It is evidence that the nightclub act we debuted in 1965 was by now extra smooth, and we sounded super cool and confident. Both Flo and I also had featured comedy bits and some lead singing.

Of the twenty tracks recorded for the cancelled album, there were several songs we had sung at the Copacabana in 1965. We also did a medley of songs from *I Hear A Symphony*, including "With A Song In My Heart," "Stranger In Paradise," and "Wonderful, Wonderful." These were some of Diane's shining moments on the super ballads; I think her acting really showed.

One of the most magical moments captured on the audio tape was Flo's strong lead vocals on the song "People", from the Broadway musical *Funny Girl* (1963). I also had my own solo in the middle of the song as well. There was enough new material to warrant a full "live" album release, and these tracks from the Roostertail really showcase our trademark three-part harmonies.

From September 29 to October 19, The Supremes headlined The Frontier in Las Vegas, Nevada, which was later to become one of our regular gigs. Diane and Berry were now officially "an item." This gave Diane even greater influence with Berry and made Florence feel more left out, so she spent a lot of time in her room calling home. This was the era in which Flo was visibly declining. Although Florence was not much of a gambler, Diane, Berry, and I fully embraced the fun of Vegas, and when we weren't performing we could very often be found in the casino. Diane always won, as she would throw up a hundred dollars and win it. I was too "chicken" to do that. I would stay up all night just playing. Once I won enough to buy my Rolls Royce, but that was a few years later when I got more nerve and more gambling skill.

October 1966 was a whirlwind of activity. We were busy in the studio recording twenty-four tracks for our forthcoming album tribute to the songwriters Richard Rodgers and Lorenz Hart. On November 12, Motown released our next single, "You Keep Me Hangin' On," which raced up the charts to become our eighth No. 1 hit. We went back on *The Ed Sullivan Show* to perform it.

On December 4, we returned to *The Ed Sullivan Show*. This time, we performed "My Favorite Things" from our *Merry Christmas* album, as well as a medley of our hits. We were wearing our Loretta Young-style yellow chiffon gowns, and performed Cholly Atkin's choreography. Although Flo was at an emotional low by this point, for this particular show she glowed. That same month, we also returned to the local Detroit television show *Swingin' Time*. Then it was off to Miami for another Christmas season headlining at the Eden Roc Hotel. The Eden Roc and Deauville Hotels were always great to play because most of the Jewish families came down for spring breaks, and we always performed during the holiday seasons. Miami Beach was so much fun in those days, as was the El San Juan Hotel in Puerto Rico.

In January 1967, we began recording songs for a forthcoming album called *The Supremes Sing Disney Classics*. Unfortunately, the album was never released in its entirety. Three of these tracks were released in 1987 on the compilation album *The Never-Before-Released Masters*.

Below and bottom: Flo, Diane, and I have fun dressing up in the different gold clothing. Flo shines in particular, with her haughtiness and statuesque beauty. A group portrait from this shoot appeared on the front cover of the program for "An Evening with The Supremes" (1966).

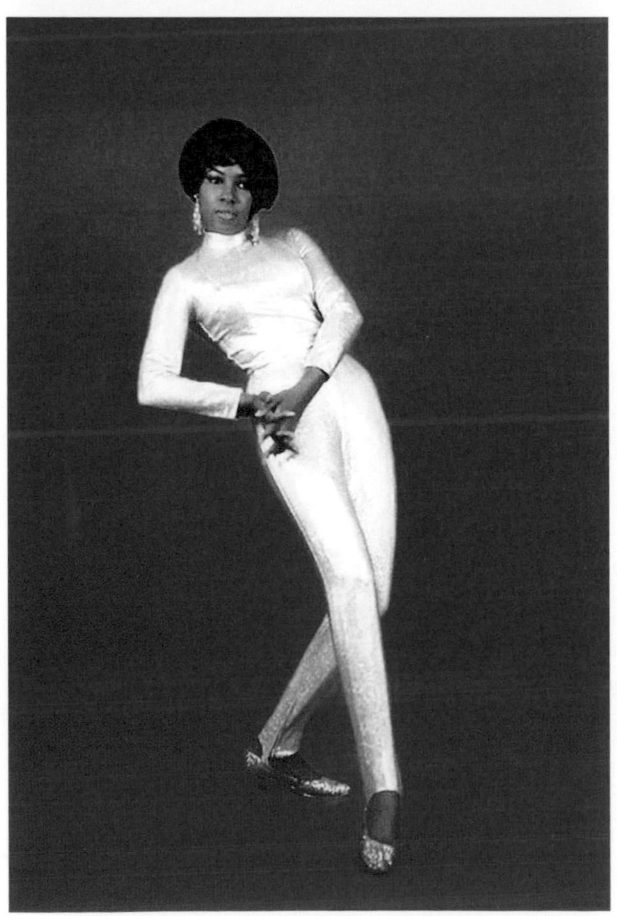

Some of the Disney songs that Flo, Diane, and I recorded that month included "When You Wish Upon A Star" (1940), "Whistle While You Work" (1937), and "Supercalifragilisticexpialidocious" (1964). I sang "The Ballad Of Davy Crockett" (1955), and had so much fun in the studio doing that number. On "Whistle While You Work," Diane challenged us to show off our whistling skills. I am heard making my attempt, and then complaining that my bubble gum was getting in the way. When she asks Florence to whistle, Flo replies, "No darling, I'm too busy digging this drummer, honey!"

That was pure Florence. Her sense of humor, candor, and off-the-cuff sincerity made her a true original. She and I played against each other so well, and the three of us had a lot of fun recording the playful Disney songs.

The Andrews Sisters had performed together for three decades, and I was hoping that my adventure with Flo and Diane would continue forever. However, I could see that the friendship between the three of us had developed a new dynamic. In fact, it was no longer the three of us. It was Diane and Berry on one side, and me and Flo on the other. Although there were conflicts in the group, we three still loved each other.

On January 11, 1967, our latest single, "Love Is Here And Now You're Gone," was released. This was our ninth No. 1 single, and the third in a row on our current winning streak. On January 22, we were the guest stars on *The Andy Williams Show*, and our album *The Supremes Sing Holland-Dozier-Holland* was released. It made it to No. 6 in *Billboard*.

At the beginning of the year, we headlined Elmwood Casino in Windsor, Canada, and were in Detroit for another engagement at the Roostertail club. Now we were the darlings of the press, and we were written about constantly. *Soul* magazine ran a cover story called "Good Things Come in Threes," and *Playboy* published its annual readers' poll. It declared that The Supremes were the number one musical group, followed by The Beatles, and Peter, Paul & Mary.

That year, the rock 'n' roll magazine *Hit Parade* glowingly reported, "The Supremes are the female equivalent of The Beatles. They are also Beatles fans...which Beatle do they like best? Diana: 'All four. I love them as a group sound.' Mary: 'Me, ditto!' Florence: 'George, he's so dreamy looking.'"

On March 2, the television special *Rodgers & Hart Today* was broadcast. The Supremes shared the stage with Petula Clark, Bobby Darin, Count Basie, and The Mamas & The Papas. The musical director was none other than Quincy Jones.

Our new release in March, "The Happening," was the theme song for a film of the same name, starring Anthony Quinn, Michael Parks, George Maharis, Martha Hyer, and Faye Dunaway. The single shot to the top of the charts, becoming our tenth No. 1 hit.

While all of this success was happening, sadly we were falling apart internally. The Motown machinery was fast positioning Diane out front as a soloist. We noticed that the television cameras were no longer on the three of us, but focused on Diane. Sometimes, social events would come up, and Florence and I didn't even know about them until they were over. New York-based writer Earl Wilson was one of the first gossip columnists to write about what was happening to the group. In early 1967, when it came to light that plans were under way to change our name to "Diana Ross & The Supremes," the die was cast.

So, one of my best friends was moving into the limelight, and the other was falling to pieces before my very eyes. In the beginning, Florence had been a great singer. But after being relegated to a background singer, she didn't grow vocally. In addition, Diane was progressively moving out front in the act and was given Flo's solo on the song "People." When Berry came to tell me that he wanted to change our name, he said, "Mary, you can get more money for the group as two attractions." For Florence, this was the last straw. It was like waving a red cape in front of a charging bull. Up to this point, Flo had remained silent about her growing discontent. She had kept her unhappiness inside for the past five years, but it had been eating away at her all this time. Flo needed support, but instead she received frequent reminders to stay in line.

This was not only a major crisis for Flo personally; it was also a turning point for The Supremes. Had the dream ended? Whenever we had faced a crisis before, I had always been in the middle. I am someone who remains calm amid chaos. I am also someone who walks in their own space, so I could see that I could not fix this situation: it was just not in my space of knowledge or experience.

We model full Supremes regalia on this shoot, with sequin gowns, beehive hairstyles, and lots of eye makeup. It was one of Flo's last photo sessions with us.

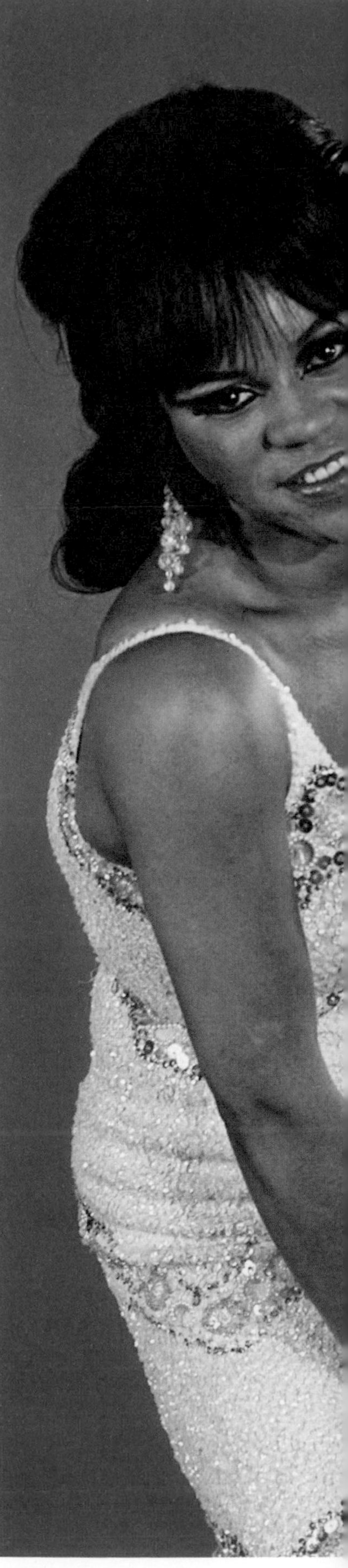

Flo had never properly dealt with being abused as a teenager, and now fear and depression were taking over her life. Florence's behavior had become more erratic over the past few years. She could no longer hide her hurt and pain. While Diane and I loved "the life" and the constant touring, Flo did not. She was more the type to miss her home and family. She racked up hundreds of dollars in telephone bills by calling her family. It all became too much for her. There were missed gigs, excessive drinking, and an increased amount of resentment toward Diane and Berry. My life became consumed with watching over and protecting Flo, and trying to keep the peace. Her pain was worse than anyone could imagine.

In April 1967, Berry Gordy called us to his house for a meeting, at which Florence was told that she would have to leave The Supremes. Flo and her mother were there at this meeting.

Mrs. Ballard said, "But Mary doesn't want Florence to leave."

True, I wanted her to stay, but I had to agree that Flo was not behaving as though she wanted to be in the group. It was decided that if Flo straightened up, she could stay. Here I was in the middle again. If Flo were to leave, Diane, Berry, and I would quickly have to find someone to replace her, even if it was only temporary.

It was Diane who said, "Hey, what about Cindy Birdsong of Patti LaBelle & The Bluebelles? Everyone says that Cindy and Florence look alike. She would be a good replacement."

While all of this was going on, I kept hoping that Florence would be able to change her attitude and cooperate with Motown's plans for Diane and for The Supremes. Personally, I loved being in the greatest female singing trio in musical history, and I wasn't willing to walk away from it all. Although I did not want Diane to leave us either, I knew this was becoming increasingly likely and that there was nothing I could do to stop it. She and I never talked about her going solo; she was with Berry now and made her plans with him. I missed both Diane and Flo so much; my heart ached for their friendship. But neither of them wanted me in their lives. Flo saw me as the enemy, on "their" side." I felt so alone.

Flo was not the type of person who was willing to stick around to see what was going to happen. It was not her decision to leave, but she didn't get the support she needed to stay. She was a fighter, and she knew how to fight back. In later life, she was labeled as being bitter about Diane and the decisions made by Motown, but being bitter was not part of Flo's nature. It was her pain speaking.

As The Supremes were booked up for months in advance, and in demand all over the world, we had to find a replacement for Flo, in case she did not show up. We contacted Cindy Birdsong to ask her if she would be willing to stand in, and she immediately agreed. Although Flo was still in the group for many of our performances, we started rehearsing with Cindy. Personally, I missed Flo so much, her laughter and her street smart ways. She was not helping herself or me.

Although I liked Cindy, I was still hoping that she wouldn't replace Flo. The sad thing was that Florence was falling deeper and deeper into her sorrow before my very eyes. In my own little way, I tried, but now I see that she needed professional help. I was going through a lot as well, trying to juggle my own life. After all, I too was being left out of things as the limelight fell on Diane.

It was on April 29 that Cindy first performed with us, for a very high-profile engagement at the Hollywood Bowl. It was so odd not to have Flo by my side, but I had to start getting used to it because it seemed that this might be the new reality. Plus, Cindy is one of the nicest human beings in the world; you had to like her. It was very sad that most people did not know that Flo was out of the group, because it was not publicized. Our fans knew, but the public could not tell the difference because Cindy looked so much like Flo.

Flo was with us in May for what was going to be her last performance on *The Ed Sullivan Show*. We performed our latest No. 1 hit, "The Happening" (1967), and a show tune medley we called "Millie/Rose/Mame," taken from the musicals *Thoroughly Modern Millie*, *Gypsy*, and *Mame*. Flo was still with us at the Copacabana, also in May. Two shows were taped there for a possible album. During this engagement, it still seemed up in the air as to whether or not Florence would be leaving.

As it turned out, it was Flo's final Copacabana engagement. (In 2018, on the expanded edition of the album *The Supremes Sing Holland-Dozier-Holland,* some of the tracks with Florence and us at the Copa were released to the public.) Throughout this time, I was a nervous wreck. No one knew how much all the upset affected me.

Here we are hanging out with our producers —Holland-Dozier-Holland—on the steps of Hitsville in 1966, in between recording sessions for a new song. Images from the same shoot were used on *The Supremes Sing Holland-Dozier-Holland*, released in January 1967.

I was into animal prints back in the day and still am to this day. It is my "Wild" side. A photo from this shoot was used on the cover of the cover album *Diana Ross & The Supremes Sing and Perform "Funny Girl,"* released in 1968.

I loved my friends Diane and Flo; I loved The Supremes and my work, but it was all falling apart. While everyone was concerned about Diane and Flo, no one asked me how I was doing.

On May 22, Motown released our tribute to the songwriters Richard Rodgers and Lorenz Hart. Titled *The Supremes Sing Rodgers & Hart* (1967), it was one of our most beautiful albums, and we all had a chance to shine on it. This was our final 1960s album to be credited to "The Supremes." It made it to No. 20 on the album charts. Although there were twenty-four songs recorded for this album, in its original release only twelve were used. I was heard sharing a duet with Diane on the song "Falling In Love With Love" (1938). Although Flo had recorded duet lead vocals with Diane on the song "Manhattan" (1925), it was one of the songs that remained "in the can." Finally, in 1987 and again in 2002, our Rodgers & Hart album was released with all twenty-four studio tracks intact.

Florence continued to tour with us on and off. She remained part of the group until July 1967. Then, one evening, there was a big backstage argument when Flo was about to go on stage for our Flamingo Hotel engagement in Las Vegas.

The writing was on the wall. Because Florence's problems had been getting worse, we had kept Cindy on call like an understudy. I, of course, had to teach her all of Florence's choreography, which was very painful. In fact, I felt like a thief in the night betraying my friend. Sure enough, something bad happened. Florence had never been able to hold alcohol—one beer could do the trick—and on this night she went overboard. It was the end of Flo and the beginning of Cindy in The Supremes. It was like the song we sang on our first album, "Time Changes Things (It's True)" (1962).

Ironically, tracks that featured Flo continued to appear on our albums until 1969. This included our next single, "Reflections" (1967), which was our first release under the name "Diana Ross & The Supremes." One of our most popular songs, "Reflections" made it to No. 2 on the charts in the U.S.A. "In And Out Of Love" (1967) was the last single that featured Florence. She can be heard on "What Becomes Of The Brokenhearted" and "Let The Music Play" from our 1969 album *Let The Sunshine In*, and she is also on "Blowin' In The Wind" from *Cream Of The Crop* (1969). After Flo left the group, I was not invited to sing on many of the later recordings while Diane was in the group. Hers was the only voice Motown seemed to need, and Motown's in-house backing vocalists, The Andantes, were brought in to sing on the tracks.

Socially, The Supremes were all over the map, but now with Cindy instead of Flo. In July 1967, we sung at the Presidential Ball in Las Vegas. We also met President Lyndon B. Johnson at the Cocoanut Grove in Los Angeles.

We had a full schedule of touring, too. In July, we headlined Forest Hills Stadium in Forest Hills, New York. In August, we were at the St. Moritz Hotel in New York City and at the Steel Pier in Atlantic City, New Jersey, before we headed off to Montreal, Canada, for the world's fair: Expo 67.

At the end of the month, the album *Diana Ross & The Supremes: Greatest Hits* (1967) was released. It contained all ten of our No. 1 hits, right up to "The Happening," ten of our other chart successes, and a couple of favorite "B" sides. The album shot straight to No. 1 on the *Billboard* album chart and became our biggest-selling album. The package was the most deluxe album we had ever released. With a beautiful sketch of Flo, Diane, and me on the cover, in a sea of blue, it was incredibly classy. As a special bonus, the album also had a pull-out insert that featured gorgeous artistic portraits of the three of us, created by artist Robert Taylor.

Famed Broadway actress Carol Channing wrote the liner notes to our *Greatest Hits* album. In them she said, "I first opened in *Hello Dolly!* on November 18, 1963, in the Motor Town. And that was about the time Diana, Florence, and Mary started to make that Motown Sound famous around the world...Great as The Supremes are on records; they are even greater in person."

We returned to television's *The Hollywood Palace* in September. This marked Cindy's national television debut with The Supremes. The host that evening was our dear friend Sammy Davis Jr. How great was the feeling of working with one of my heroes? Fantastic! We sang our latest hit "Reflections" and the Rodgers & Hart classic "The Lady Is A Tramp" (1937) in a medley with "Let's Get Away From It All" (1941). We were then joined by Sammy for "Under Paris Skies" (1951) and some comedy bits. It was also on that episode of *The Hollywood Palace* that I debuted my new blond look. From October 2 to 16, we headlined The Cave in Vancouver, Canada.

In 1967, we go back to our roots to the Brewster-Douglass public housing project in Detroit to film a promotion fundraising film for the United Fund. This photo featured in an article about us in the *Detroit Free Press* on July 30, 1967.

Diane strikes a dynamic pose for this studio portrait, flanked by myself and Cindy. Our spectacular wardrobe was a major expense. These gowns are currently with the Motown Museum.

Below and bottom: In August 1967 we returned to Detroit to play the popular Roostertail. It is Cindy's debut performance at the nightclub. Motown recorded the show for a possible live album that was never released.

In this image by celebrity photographer James Kriegsmann, Cindy, Diane, and I wear the heavily embellished "Chandelier" gowns, designed in 1967 by Michael Travis. Sadly, the dresses were among several sets of costumes destroyed in a fire in Mexico City in 1974.

Cindy, Diane, and I wore these two-piece gowns designed by Michael Travis for an appearance on *The Tennessee Ernie Ford Special* (1967), where we sang "Old Mill Stream Medley." We also wore them on *The Ed Sullivan Show* in May 1968 when we sang "Happy Birthday" to Irving Berlin. The gowns were accessorized with a large hat and umbrella, and the skirts could be removed to reveal a leotard swim suit.

Wedged in between more tour dates, we went to Mexico in October 1967 to tape our acting roles as missionary nuns on an episode of the popular television show *Tarzan*. It was something of a departure for us to play nuns. Our particular episode was called "The Convert." Naturally, much of our time on camera was spent singing. I fell in love with acting at this time and knew that one day I would do some more. In one scene, fire broke out and I screamed really loudly. Someone yelled "CUT!" Berry came over and told me not to scream again. As nuns, we performed the songs "The Lord Helps Those Who Help Themselves" and "Michael Row The Boat Ashore." We all had dialogue and several nice close-ups, but Diane, I found out while shooting, was "the star" of the show. That was cool, though, because I loved being on set in my first acting role, even though it was a supporting one. Ron Ely, who played the title role of *Tarzan*, was delightful to work with. There is a great picture of us in the streets of Mexico City with Ron, which was used on the cover of one of our later CDs. We all had a ball during the recording, and I absolutely loved it, even though I nearly drowned while we were filming one scene, as I never learned how to swim!

On October 25, our latest single "In And Out Of Love" (1967) was released. Making it to No. 9 on the charts, it had the distinction of being our thirteenth Top 10 hit in the last three years. Every one of those songs was written and produced by Holland-Dozier-Holland, and this one represented our final work with them.

In the October 10 edition of his nationally distributed gossip column, our friend Earl Wilson reported: "Secret Stuff: The Supremes are still disturbed over the continuing feud between Diana Ross and former member Florence Ballard." It was clear that The Supremes were suffering in more ways than one, but life went on. We had concerts in Washington, Oregon, and California, and more television appearances. In November, we were on *The Ed Sullivan Show* alongside The Temptations, and we sang our latest hit "In And Out Of Love." Later in the show, we appeared with The Temptations on a brightly colored stage to perform a medley of their hits, and they sang a medley of ours. It was great fun to perform with them. In fact, we worked so well together that, over the next two years, we recorded two studio albums and starred in two television specials with The Temptations. We had achieved so many "firsts" as The Supremes. As singers, we had opened many doors for other artists. Now, here we were about to be one of the first rock 'n' rollers to have our own television special, with our brothers The Temptations!

On December 3, we were guest stars on *The Tennessee Ernie Ford Special*. On that particular program, we sang "Reflections," "The Happening," and a medley of old-time songs. It still seemed odd not to have Flo with us, since she sang on all of these recordings. I simply had to get used to it. Michael Travis designed two-piece beige lace gowns for us to wear with huge hats and break-away skirts. When we removed the skirts, it revealed a bathing suit-like bodysuit. This was one of the times when the television shows commissioned gowns to be designed and made especially for us. The result was one of our sexiest looks in high fashion, and the beginning of our designer gown era.

Overall, the year 1967 was one of challenges and changes for me, Flo, and for The Supremes. Although Florence was no longer in the group, it was her talent and energy that had helped make The Supremes as successful and popular as we were. We were three little black girls who had dared to dream, and the whole world had watched as we made our dreams come true.

As 1968 started, Cindy, Diane, and I went off to Europe for a six-week schedule of television shows, concerts, and high-profile socializing, during which time I learned that money does not necessarily make you happy. First was Milan, then London, where we had lunch with the Duke and Duchess of Bedford. The next stop was Paris, where we appeared on the television show *Claude Francois' Studio 102*. While we were in Europe, the *Tarzan* episode we starred in—"The Convert"—aired in the U.S.A. Then we went to Germany to do our entire nightclub act for a television special, *The Supremes in Berlin*.

In Amsterdam, our nightclub appearance was again filmed and broadcast as a television special. It has since been released as a DVD with the title *The Supremes: Greatest Hits—Live in Amsterdam*. The DVD features three "bonus" performances of us with Florence, taken from our earlier 1964 performance there. Next, it was on to Madrid for another television special, then the same thing the next day in Paris.

While in Europe, we were booked to perform at the Bambi Awards ceremony—the equivalent

Cindy makes her debut on *The Ed Sullivan Show* in November 1967 performing "In And Out Of Love." The gowns were designed by LaVetta of Beverly Hills, who said she was inspired by the choir robes worn by altar boys in church.

Below and opposite: Diane, Cindy and I model a set of black and white gowns, which I loved as the vertical stripes made me look taller. These were designed by Tee-Ca's of New York and originally worn when Flo was in the group. We wore these dresses when we performed live at the Michigan State Fair in 1967. Sadly they are now missing from my collection and in the collection of the Hard Rock Café.

Here, Diane, Cindy, and I match every element of our look: pink gowns, pink shoes, pink earrings, and pink lipstick. I loved those pink earrings. These gowns were designed by James Galanos. The outfits appear on the front cover of *Diana Ross & The Supremes Sing & Perform Funny Girl* (1968).

of the Academy Awards—in Munich, Germany. The stars really came out for this event. How thrilling for us to be among the likes of Elizabeth Taylor, Richard Burton, Johnny Weissmuller, and Tom Jones. It is universally known that Tom Jones loved the ladies, but I had no idea that he secretly had his eye on me! My agent told me that Tom was going to be at the Bambi show, and that he wanted to meet me! My relationship with Tom is one I will never forget. The tabloids had a field day with our love affair, which demonstrated how the times were changing back then. Now, we are friends for life.

For The Supremes, it was on to France to the annual MIDEM Festival in Cannes. While there, we performed our latest single "In And Out Of Love." During this trip, we also went to Geneva to do a television show.

Next came the glitziest European gig of the trip: from January to February 1968, we headlined at the chic London nightclub the Talk of the Town. On our way to London, we saw in an airplane magazine that one of our favorite stars, Ms. Lena Horne, was closing her engagement the night before we were to open. We begged Berry to get tickets for us to see her. By now, we were calling him "Berry" and not the usual "Mr. Gordy." Were we surprised when he told us he knew Lena? Absolutely! When we arrived at the club the next evening, the paparazzi were there and took loads of photographs of us. Yes, even in the late 1960s, the paparazzi were following us around.

Ms. Lena was fabulous, and after her show we went backstage to her dressing room. She was so gracious and kind, and we stayed for over an hour, drinking champagne and talking about life.

Our opening night was a huge event. The shows were taped and became our second most famous live album. Afterward, the Duke and Duchess of Bedford threw a party in our honor at the Club Dell' Aretusa in Chelsea. The guests that evening included Mick Jagger, Marianne Faithfull, Lynn Redgrave, Cindy's favorite actor Michael Caine, and my new friend Tom Jones.

During the 1960s, England had become a second home for us. While in London, we appeared on the *Sunday Night at the London Palladium* television show. In February 1968, the BBC broadcast an hour-long special starring us, titled *The Supremes: Live at London's Talk of the Town*. And we were also guests on *The Eamonn Andrews Show* in London.

Back in Detroit, on February 24, I went into the studio and recorded one of my rare solo songs from this era of The Supremes. It was the pop ballad "Can't Take My Eyes Off Of You," and it was released in several formats over the years.

Our busy schedule continued with a trip to New York to appear on *The Ed Sullivan Show*. This time we performed "Forever Came Today" (1968) and a medley of songs by Fats Waller, which included "Honeysuckle Rose," "Ain't Misbehavin'" (both 1929), and "Keeping Out Of Mischief Now" (1932). Also on the show were Nancy Sinatra, Lee Hazlewood, and Spanky & Our Gang.

On March 28, we opened at the Copacabana for another lengthy visit. The performances were going well until April 4, when we learned that Dr. Martin Luther King had been shot in Memphis, Tennessee. We immediately cut short our engagement. The following night, we appeared on *The Tonight Show*, performing our version of the song "Somewhere" from *West Side Story* (1957). Instead of the original spoken part that had been written by Maurice King, which Diane delivered in the middle of the song, a new section was written as a message of peace, in the words of Dr. Martin Luther King. We drew even wider acceptance with this performance, and the newly included quote became a regular part of our rendition of "Somewhere."

We then flew to Atlanta to attend the funeral of Dr. Martin Luther King. We were there with all the stars, including Lena Horne, Sammy Davis Jr., Sidney Poitier, and Harry Belafonte. All of the prominent black figures were present, too, such as Rosa Parks, Andrew Young, John Lewis, Jesse Jackson, and Miss Aretha Franklin, who sang so beautifully at the funeral. This was indeed a very sad day. (As I write this on August 31, 2018, it is another sad day as we have just put Aretha Franklin to rest and celebrated her life.)

Around the world, we were acknowledged as stars who were treated as equals. But in the U.S.A., it was still very bad for most blacks. Dr. Martin Luther King's funeral was especially sad as he had stood up for the equality of everyone, and now he was gone.

One evening, a Jewish lady came up to me after one of our shows in Miami, when we were playing at the Eden Roc Hotel in 1968, and she said, "You girls are so wonderful. I let my whole family stay up and watch you every Sunday night on *The Ed Sullivan Show*." My brother—who

Below and opposite: We perform live at the Michigan State Fair in 1967, accompanied by the Jimmy Wilkins band. I loved the pink gowns (opposite) as they reminded me of Loretta Young. Unfortunately they are among several sets that went missing from my storage boxes.

considered himself a "Black Panther wannabe"—said to me, "Mary, what does she mean she lets her whole family watch you?" But here in America, that's the way the racial climate was in the 1960s, even after the Civil Rights bill had been passed.

After the funeral, we continued our jet-setting life. Diane and I were now major stars, so we found ourselves performing with some of the biggest names in show business. In May, Diana Ross & The Supremes were part of the eightieth birthday celebrations of songwriter Irving Berlin, appearing on a special edition of *The Ed Sullivan Show*. The three of us, now with Cindy of course, sang the song "Always" (1925), and we also joined Ethel Merman for a medley of Berlin's songwriting hits, including "Say It With Music" (1921), "It's A Lovely Day Today" (1950), "Heat Wave" (1933), and "Say It Isn't So" (1932). Other guests on the show were Bing Crosby, Bob Hope, Harry James, and Robert Goulet.

I have always admired great songwriters. We had saluted Richard Rodgers with our Top 20 Rodgers & Hart album, and we had celebrated Irving Berlin on *The Ed Sullivan Show*, but it was Holland-Dozier-Holland who made us famous.

Unfortunately, there was some serious trouble brewing at Motown. Our producers, Holland-Dozier-Holland, became very unhappy with the way Motown was being run, and also with their rate of compensation.

Later in the year, in August 1968, Motown sued Brian Holland, Lamont Dozier, and Eddie Holland for $4 million for failing to work. Holland-Dozier-Holland counter-sued Motown for $22 million, in a case that dragged on for years.

Holland-Dozier-Holland eventually established their own record company, Invictus/Hot Wax Records, and produced several huge hits of their own. One of their most successful groups was a female trio called Honey Cone. They also signed my dear friend Freda Payne, and produced her trademark song "Band Of Gold" (1970).

After losing Holland-Dozier-Holland and releasing several records that didn't do well, the people at Motown were getting very concerned. They had to try and find new producers for us, to come up with a hit.

Florence, meanwhile, was having problems with Motown Records, too. In February 1968, she had signed the papers to dissolve her contract with the label. Seven days later, she married Tommy Chapman, who at one point had been our chauffeur. If she was happy, I was happy for her. Flo was going forward with her newly launched solo career, which included a short-lived recording contract with ABC Records. I hoped that she would be able to make a name for herself away from The Supremes. She was certainly talented enough to produce hit records, and even go into the movies. If Pearl Bailey could succeed with her bawdy and outspoken personality, why not Florence? She appeared on television shows such as *Swingin' Time*, where she performed her debut solo single "It Doesn't Matter How You Say It" (1968). Then she released another single, which was written by future disco hit-maker Van McCoy, called "Love Ain't Love" (1968).

The Motown machinery was still releasing The Supremes albums, including *Live at London's Talk of the Town* and *Diana Ross & The Supremes Sing and Perform "Funny Girl"* (both 1968). Because these were novelty albums, and we hadn't had a big hit single that year, neither of them did well. The live album made it to No. 57 in *Billboard*, and the *Funny Girl* tribute only made it to No. 150.

At this time, I was absolutely exhausted and decided to take a well-needed vacation. I felt that no one cared about me because everyone was so busy making arrangements for Diane's inevitable departure from the group and her new solo career. It was like I did not exist. Wouldn't you know it, they set a date to record a great song at the exact same time I would be on vacation. My vocals were no longer a prerequisite for a Supremes hit, and I was very hurt. That was one of those times when I rebelled. And, boy did it cost me!

The loss of Holland-Dozier-Holland was causing us to slip on the music charts. So, the task of creating a hit single was given to new producers, who came up with "Love Child" (1968). The subject matter of the song concerned the social stigma of being an "illegitimate" child. It was a departure for a Supremes single, because it had lots of social consciousness, and it instantly grabbed people's attention.

The night before the single was released, we appeared on *The Ed Sullivan Show*, with a radically different look. When we performed "Love Child," instead of being dressed glamorously in our usual elaborate beaded and sequined gowns, we were clad in very casual street clothes. Diane was wearing cut-off jeans, and her sweatshirt had the words "Love Child" written

This studio portrait shows Cindy, Diane, and me wearing blue chiffon gowns with lovely little white daisy flowers. The Grecian-inspired design is very ladylike, with powder-blue earrings and matching shoes. I am wearing my 4-carat heart-shaped diamond and dome-shaped rings.

Here I am wearing my Doris Day-inspired blond wig for a relaxed photo shoot with Cindy and Diane in Mexico in 1967.

We were the first pop group to have our own television special, *T.C.B.*, on NBC in 1968. Wearing the Michael Travis "Butterfly" gowns we perform in front of a live audience on a very high Plexiglas stage with a large orchestra behind us.

across it. We had taken our latest song into sheer theater. Everyone was talking about this controversial performance. The single zoomed up the charts, and The Supremes were back at No. 1. But I wasn't even on the recording. I was devastated! It was like a Milli Vanilli moment, where I was on television lip-syncing to someone else's voice. I felt so "cheap." It was right then that I knew I had to start looking out for myself.

Earlier, when Flo was about to be put out of the group, she had said to me, "One day they will do it to you Mary." I felt like that day had arrived. When the accompanying *Love Child* (1968) album was released, it made it to No. 19 on the charts. All of a sudden, we weren't just the stunningly dressed classy Supremes, we were now the "socially conscious Supremes!" But I felt like a fraud, even though we were making history and doing great things.

I loved appearing on the *Bing Crosby Special: Making Movies* with Bob Hope and José Feliciano, which aired in October. It was filmed on Western movie sets and had something of a Wild West theme to it. At one point in the show, Cindy, Diane, and I were filmed wearing cowgirl gear and singing "The Ballad Of High Noon (Do Not Forsake Me)," from the film *High Noon* (1952). We also performed a medley of songs from *Paint Your Wagon* (1951), with Bing.

In early November, we performed at Berns in Stockholm, Sweden. We had an absolute blast while we were there. Our presence in Stockholm was highly publicized, and one night we even attracted the Crown Prince and his sister, Crown Princess Christina. It just so happened that Princess Christina was around the same age as us, and she was a true Supremes fan. She had to bring her younger brother as her escort, but they came to see our show several times, and we became fast friends with Princess Christina. I was thrilled to see that Mrs. Powell's prediction was coming true: "One day, you girls will be singing before kings and queens."

Years later, in 1997, Princess Christina came to the Hamburger Börs, Stockholm, when I was starring in the theatrical show *Supreme Soul* with Tommy Nilsson, and she threw our closing night party. It was during this engagement that my mother, Johnnie Mae, passed. Princess Christina led the whole audience in a cheer to my mom.

From Stockholm we went on to Copenhagen, Denmark; Malmö, Sweden; and Brussels, Belgium. Next, it was back to London, where we appeared at the Royal Variety Performance, with members of the Royal Family in attendance, including the Queen Mother, Princess Margaret, Prince Charles, and Princess Anne. While we were in the greeting line to meet the Royal Family, the Queen's sister, Princess Margaret, loudly said to me, "Is that a wig you are wearing, Mary?"

I had no idea how to react to that! This was not a question that one lady asks another at a formal function! It was so unexpected. And in the newspapers the next day, there was a photograph of us that was not pretty. It looked like I wanted to kill Princess Margaret. I learned a big lesson that time. Apparently, just because you are royalty, it doesn't necessarily mean that you have good manners!

One of the best things that resulted from our early 1968 sales slump was that Motown came up with a new plan for our careers: teaming us up for a series of albums with The Temptations. Putting together Motown's biggest female group with its biggest male group made perfect sense. However, two key figures of our groups, Florence Ballard and David Ruffin, were not there to share in this triumph.

Our first of four group duet albums with the guys was titled *Diana Ross & The Supremes Join The Temptations* (1968). It contained the hit single "I'm Gonna Make You Love Me" (1968), and both the album and the single made it to No. 2 on the respective *Billboard* charts. This returned us to form, in terms of sales.

However, the biggest project of the year for us was our top-rated television special *T.C.B.*, which stands for "Taking Care of Business." An hour-long program, it was essentially a concert special for both groups. We wore a stunning new array of sequin-covered gowns, and The Temptations were clad in Edwardian-style matching green suits—it really was a dazzling show. It was at this time that designers started bringing us their fabulous sketches for our gowns. Michael Travis designed all of the wonderful outfits that The Supremes and The Temptations wore on this show, and he became our personal designer. He is responsible for some of our most beautiful and elaborate dresses from this era, which are now in my Mary Wilson Collection.

Cindy and I, along with Eddie Kendricks and Otis Williams of The Temptations, also recorded our own featured number for the special. It was

SUPREMES
TEMPTATIONS
DIANA ROSS
SUPREMES
TEMPTATIONS
SUPREMES
TEMPTATIONS
SUPREMES
TEMPTATIONS

We perform "I'm Losing You" as part of a medley of hits with The Temptations on *The Ed Sullivan Show* in November 1967. Being on Ed's show with our "brothers" The Temptations was a "dream come true" for us.

a version of the Sérgio Mendes 1966 hit song "Mas, Que Nada." Unfortunately, it never made it onto the show.

Despite this, the television special was a huge success, and the soundtrack album from it, also called *T.C.B.*, zoomed up the charts almost instantly, to hit No. 1 in *Billboard*. It was the perfect way to end 1968: back on top!

"Love Child" was such a big hit that Motown sought to release a follow-up song with the same kind of pathos and drama in the lyrics. They came up with "I'm Livin' In Shame" (1969), which was a Top 10 hit. On January 5, we appeared on *The Ed Sullivan Show*, reprising "Love Child" and introducing "I'm Livin' In Shame" to a national audience. Again, I was not on this song. I know that actors do some of their best work only to have it end up on the cutting room floor when editors and producers get their hands on it, but I wasn't even on the floor any more! It was like I no longer existed.

However, I was still in the studio, recording. In addition to several tour dates in the Midwest, we went back in the studio in January 1969. We recorded renditions of recent hits "Everyday People" and "Hey Jude," and I recorded Dusty Springfield's "Son Of A Preacher Man" (all 1969). Our single with The Temptations, "I'm Gonna Make You Love Me" hit the Top 10 on the U.K.'s *Top of the Pops* list for 1969. There were also two more U.K.-only singles with The Temptations: "I Second That Emotion" (1969) and "Why (Must We Fall In Love)" (1970).

At the beginning of 1969, we headlined The Frontier in Las Vegas and were co-stars on *The Bob Hope Special*. We were also the hosts of the television variety show *The Hollywood Palace*, and appeared on *The Tonight Show*. Meanwhile, Motown continued to release more Top 40 Supremes hits, including "The Composer," "No Matter What Sign You Are," and, with The Temptations, "I'll Try Something New" (all 1969).

My fast-paced life continued non-stop. April found us headlining at the Casanova Room at the Deauville Hotel in Miami. In May, we were back on *The Ed Sullivan Show* performing the astrology themed song "No Matter What Sign You Are" (1969), and Motown released our next Diana Ross & The Supremes album, *Let The Sunshine In* (1969).

"Top secret" plans were unfolding for Diane's exit from the group, and also for The Supremes to find a replacement for her so we could continue to release albums on Motown. There were lots of singers being considered as Diane's replacement; even I was looking. Actually, this was a time when I did not know what I was going to do. Would I stay with the group, or leave? However, one scenario—the possibility of Syreeta Wright joining The Supremes—was shelved when Berry Gordy met prize boxer Ernie Terrell and saw his sister, Jean Terrell, performing in a nightclub in Florida. Mr. Gordy was instantly impressed.

Jean was signed to Motown on her own contract. Berry came to me and said, "I have found a girl who I think can replace Diana." Although I was cautious, as soon as I met Jean Terrell and heard her sing, I knew she was going to work well in the group. She had a similar sounding voice to Diane, but very different in style, and she was very soulful, which for me was great. It was going to be a new era for The Supremes, and I was happy and relieved to see that everything was going to work out. With Jean, we had a good chance of winning the battle to keep The Supremes on top. It took me years to get over losing both Diane and Florence, but Jean being in the group gave me new hope. I could stop worrying about my future.

Although the lineup of The '70s Supremes was yet to be finalized, on June 23 Jean recorded her solo lead vocal to the song "Take A Closer Look At Me," with Frank Wilson producing. It was undecided if she would be a solo act. Cindy and I were ultimately to add our vocals later. The '70s Supremes debut album was already officially under way! However, Diane, Cindy, and I were still touring as Diana Ross & The Supremes. We appeared at the Carter Barron Amphitheatre, in Washington, D.C., where we hung out with several prominent politicians, including Senator Ted Kennedy. Next, at the Carousel Theater in Framingham, Massachusetts, we had Stevie Wonder opening for us. Then, it was back to the recording studio with "our guys" The Temptations.

We were in London on the television show *Top of the Pops* on July 31. The other guests on the program were The Rolling Stones, Donovan, Billy Preston, and Cilla Black.

Motown's latest discovery, The Jackson 5, opened for us at The Forum in Inglewood, California, in August. That month, our version of the rock group The Band's "The Weight," which we recorded with The Temptations, was released, followed in September by our second studio

These embellished gowns were designed by LaVetta of Beverly Hills and sometimes worn with the "LaVetta Delight" coats (1968). They are among those now missing from my collection.

Below and bottom: *The Hollywood Palace* television show was such fun, and we hosted it several times. On this occasion one of our favorite entertainers, Sammy Davis Jr., is hosting. Diane performs a song-and-dance tribute to Fred Astaire and Ginger Rogers movie musicals with him (bottom left). The show was broadcast on 18 October 1969.

album with the guys, *Together* (1969). This album was a lot of fun to work on, and the tracks reflected this. We recorded several Motown songs such as "Stubborn Kind Of Fellow" (1962) and "Ain't Nothing Like The Real Thing" (1968), as well as covers of current hits, including Sly & The Family Stone's "Sing A Simple Song" (1968). As a special treat, my rendition of the song "Can't Take My Eyes Off Of You" appears on the album as a duet with Eddie Kendricks. I had been singing the song for a while in our act. It was really great to record it as a duet with Eddie. He was, without a doubt, one of the best tenors in the music business. The album went to No. 28 on the *Billboard* chart.

I instantly liked working with Frank Wilson as our producer. After having Holland-Dozier-Holland as producers on the vast majority of The Supremes' songs over the past few years, working with someone else was a whole new experience. Frank brought with him a West Coast kind of vibe that we were not used to having in the studio. That in itself was exciting.

It was also refreshing to be working with someone who was actively listening to my voice, and arranging things so that I sounded my best. Talking about me recording this song, Frank explained, "On 'Can't Take My Eyes Off Of You,' Mary had a real sultry, warm voice, and with that particular song, I just believed she would do a great job, and it was part of my 'modus operandi' to advance as much as possible creatively." I didn't realize it at the time, but Frank was going to be a crucial part of launching The "new" Supremes in the 1970s.

While the first "new" Supremes album was being planned, Motown had long been searching for a first solo single for Diane. One of the songs that was suggested was something that Johnny Bristol had produced called "Someday We'll Be Together" (1961). However, when Berry Gordy heard it he said, "That is perfect as Diana Ross & The Supremes' last single." Johnny had already put the backing vocals and his voice on it as a guide for Diane's lead. So, it was decided that it would be our next single—without any of The Supremes on it. Did anyone ask me to add my voice to it? No!

Our version of "Someday We'll Be Together" hit the record stores on October 12, and it zoomed up to No. 1. This was the song that epitomized the end of Diana Ross & The Supremes and became our trademark anthem. Motown indeed found the perfect song to announce the split of Diane from The Supremes; however, yet again I was not on it. Talk about a slap in the face! If ever I should have been disenchanted with The Supremes, it was now.

We were the hosts on *The Hollywood Palace* for the last time on October 18, 1969. There, we sang "Someday We'll Be Together," and The Jackson 5 also made their national television debut. They were so great that Motown was looking for a way to launch them. It was decided that since Diane was the reigning female star at that time, she would be the perfect person to introduce the public to The Jackson 5. So, a huge party was thrown at the Beverly Hills nightclub, The Daisy, in their honor. I received my invitation to the event via the same Western Union telegram invite as everyone else. (Western Union was the equivalent of today's texts.)

In the November 2 issue of the *Detroit Free Press*, entertainment editor Bob Talbert broke the news that Diane would officially leave The Supremes in January 1970, and that The Supremes would carry on with our newest addition, Jean Terrell. Finally, everyone in the world was told what was happening. It came as something of a relief that everyone now knew what was about to transpire—including me!

In the *Detroit Free Press*, it was front page news. Under a headline reading: "Supremes' Diana Ross Aims at Movie, Broadway Career," Talbert reported, "Singer Diana Ross will launch a new career as a solo performer, and Motown's most successful group, The Supremes, will get a new face and voice in January, the *Free Press* has learned...Miss [Jean] Terrell has already joined the other two Supremes—Mary Wilson and Cindy Birdsong—and the three are 'presently getting an act together.'"

Our album *Cream of the Crop* (1969) was released, and featured "Someday We'll Be Together" as the centerpiece and various Supremes tracks from different eras. The album was very eclectic, in that it even included me and Florence singing the backgrounds together on Bob Dylan's "Blowing In The Wind," which had been recorded years before in 1966. The album made it to No. 33 in *Billboard*.

The soundtrack album from our television program *G.I.T. On Broadway*, with The Temptations, featured us performing musical numbers and skits based on famous Broadway songs. Like

T.C.B. before it, this special was another hour-long song fest. We had so much fun acting the roles of Native American Indians, while The Temptations—dressed as singing Canadian Mounties—spoofed Jeanette MacDonald and Nelson Eddy. Another skit found me, with Diane and Cindy, playing waitresses in a soda shop. I loved these little acting bits. Naturally, there was also a lot of glamour, especially on the big production numbers. For this television special, Bob Mackie was the designer, and he dressed us all in beautiful costumes.

Every other month of the year, there was a new Supremes album in the record shops. Just in time for Christmas, Motown released *Diana Ross & The Supremes Greatest Hits, Volume III*. There was *Let the Sunshine In*, our album *Together* with The Temptations, *Cream of the Crop*, and the soundtrack to *G.I.T. On Broadway*. Combined with our highly publicized break-up, you could not miss The Supremes in the news!

On December 21, 1969, we were on *The Ed Sullivan Show*. It was the last time I performed on Ed's show with Diane.

The end of 1969 and the beginning of 1970 were especially hectic for me. I was actually with two groups: performing with Diane at night, and—along with Cindy—teaching Jean our stage show choreography during the day. I was juggling two different gigs at once. It took a lot of positive energy to make certain that I gave dazzling performances with Diane every night. My version of "Can't Take My Eyes Off Of You" was now part of our stage show, and every night I gave it my all.

Cindy and I worked hard with Jean, polishing our sound together and coming up with some of the best and strongest material The Supremes had been given to record in years. The "new" Supremes had to be just as exciting and glamorous as our reputation demanded, and I was up for the challenge.

Very quickly the time came for our farewell performance, at our favorite place in Las Vegas: The Frontier. The whole town was abuzz. Anyone who was anyone was there. January 14, 1970, was officially time to say goodbye to Diane.

It was our very last show with Diane, and it was a fittingly star-studded affair. The audience was full of major celebrities: Dick Clark, Wilt Chamberlain, Steve Allen, Jayne Meadows, Lou Rawls, Marvin Gaye, Smokey Robinson, and everyone from Motown. At the end of the show, several dignitaries, including the U.S. Senator from Nevada Howard Cannon, came up on stage. Then, of course we introduced Jean to the audience for the first time.

There were all sorts of telegrams and flowers sent to us. Perhaps the most touching one came from our dear friend Ed Sullivan. In his telegram, which was read on stage, he wrote: "As of tonight, one of the greatest attractions of the 1960s becomes two of the greatest attractions of the 1970s." That is exactly how I was looking at it, too.

After a night of partying and gambling with my friend Margie Haber, it was time to sleep. I was abruptly wakened by the telephone ringing. It was Berry Gordy.

After a bit of talking, he finally dropped the bomb he had called to deliver. "I don't like Jean Terrell," he said.

I sat straight up in bed and exclaimed, "What are you talking about?" I was in shock.

"I want to replace her with Syreeta Wright."

Several moments of silence ensued on the phone. "Mary, do you hear me?" he asked. "I want to replace Jean with Syreeta."

"No!" I replied without hesitation.

"All right," he said, "Then I wash my hands of the group." He hung up.

This was how the new decade was going to start? I couldn't believe it. But I was determined to stand by my decision.

Jean was not a kittenish glamour girl, but what she projected was a bold sense of self-confidence. She was exactly what The Supremes needed. I was relieved we had Jean, and I had hope for The Supremes.

Although I knew that Syreeta was a wonderful singer, I also knew she wanted a solo career. Personally, I wanted group unity for our new start. I had lost control of the group before, and I was not going to let it happen again. Unfortunately, I did not see what was in the future. I guess Berry had seen what I had not.

I found that recording with The "new" Supremes was bringing not only fresh energy and satisfaction, but also a great deal of joy. No, I was not with my friends Diane and Florence anymore, but to me this was a brand new group, a new beginning, and it felt good! Jean Terrell is such a unique singer. Watching her get behind the mike in the studio brought back memories of when I was one of The Primettes, a young girl in the studio, back on West Grand Boulevard in Detroit.

We appeared at the Frontier Hotel in Las Vegas from December 23, 1969, to January 14, 1970. Diane is here wearing a Michael Travis-designed gown that sadly was among those burned in the fire in Mexico City in 1974. On the last night, at the end of Diane's final performance as a Supreme, we introduced her replacement, Jean Terrell, to the audience. In fact, Terrell had already been recording with us for a while.

Below and opposite: We wore many of our favorite outfits for the shows at the Frontier Hotel, including the beautiful "Orange Freeze" bugle beaded jackets that were later stolen from a dressing room. The farewell performance was a particularly sad night for me. First, I lost Flo; now Diane was leaving me, too.

Cindy, Jean, and I display a more casual Western-influenced look for this group portrait. We revisited the style for the cover of our collaborative album, *The Return of the Magnificent Seven* (1971), with The Four Tops.

The "new" Supremes

1970 to 1977

y dream for myself and for The Supremes was far from over. As I look back, even though I don't think of myself as a fighter, I realize that I have had to fight all my life. The first matter of business for the 1970s was The "new" Supremes debut album with me, Cindy, and Jean. It had to be a hit! The recording process went incredibly well, and I hoped that the fans would stick with us and give the new group a chance.

What I loved the most about the *Right On* (1970) album is that all of the songs carried a universal theme of inspirational love. For this particular album, several different writers and producers were used from the Motown roster. We had Johnny Bristol, Clay McMurray, Jimmy Roach, Henry Cosby, and Al Kent, and on five of the twelve songs we worked with Frank Wilson. I think he had the best vision for how we should sound and how we should be recorded. It was truly the start of a whole new group.

Every song Frank presented to us gave us goose bumps as we recorded it. The vocal blend between the three of us worked perfectly. Jean's vocals on all of the tracks are magical. When we recorded, she had a way of riding in and around the notes with a very natural ease.

Then there was the matter of what Frank did with me and Cindy. The last two years of post-Florence Supremes, we had been buried in the music like an afterthought—or not used at all. I was an important part of the songs again, and I loved it. Even though other voices were sometimes used to fill out our sound, we were still there. Frank was always encouraging me to step into the spotlight, and he actively sought out songs that were perfect for my voice.

The "new" Supremes needed a hit record, and it was Frank who came up with our debut single, "Up The Ladder To The Roof" (1970). And what a great song it is! Frank told me that he flew to New York to find songwriter Vincent DiMarco to write our first hit. He wanted songs that would befit the reigning top female group in the world: us!

Another song that Frank produced was "Everybody's Got The Right To Love" (1970). We truly need more great songs like that. When we were recording it, I felt like we were healing the world. I will always remember the recording session for this song. I recall the joy I felt looking at both Cindy and Jean. We were not only accomplishing what we set out to do, but we were creating something quite magical.

When it was released, "Up The Ladder To The Roof" was universally accepted by fans and radio programmers alike. It shot up to No. 10 on the pop charts in *Billboard* and to No. 5 on the R&B chart. In addition, it made it to No. 6 in the U.K.

On April 26, Motown released *Right On*. The cover was a gorgeously glowing orange-toned photograph of us by Frank Dandridge. We were close together with beaming smiles on our faces. It was again one of the most elaborate packages we received. The vinyl album had a two-panel fold-out poster of me, Cindy, and Jean, in the same beautiful beaded orange floor-length gowns we wore on the front cover, looking very appropriately Supreme.

Right On sold extremely well, which made me happy. It proved that the public embraced us, and that our devoted fan base had stayed with us. We also received glowing reviews. The *All Music Guide* proclaimed, "'Up The Ladder To The Roof' opens the album with enticing voices and Frank Wilson's underappreciated first-class production...Jean Terrell brought a terrific voice and a new emotion to a group that would rack up eight Top 40 hits...it gives Mary Wilson and Cindy Birdsong a chance to use their voices to interact with Terrell, creating a true group sound. A new team, a united front...*Right On* is thoroughly enjoyable!"

To properly launch "Up The Ladder To The Roof," Jean, Cindy, and I went on *The Ed Sullivan Show*. We also performed "If My Friends Could See Me Now" from *Sweet Charity* (1966), in a medley with "Nothing Can Stop Us Now." That was exactly how I felt: back on top! Most people are not aware how celebrities, singers, and actors constantly have to re-create themselves to stay on top. If an actor loses their show, it can be scary not to know what is coming next. It is the same for a recording artist: when and where is your next hit?

One of the most exciting gigs was our return to New York City's Copacabana. Our opening night drew my dear friends Dionne Warwick, Flip Wilson, and Glen Campbell. They all came to see if the new group had the same excitement that had made us stars. The consensus was a definite "yes!" We were every bit as dazzling as Diana Ross & The Supremes had been.

In June, our next single, "Everybody's Got The Right To Love" (1970), was released. It made it to No. 21 on the pop chart and No. 11 on the R&B

The "new" Supremes embrace the 70s with Afros and plenty of gold sequins and fringing in these jumpsuits designed by Michael Travis. Cindy, Jean, and I wore these outfits on the television show *This is Tom Jones* (1970), where we sang "River Deep Mountain High" with Tom.

In the 1970s we had several fringe-type pantsuits—even the "White Rain" gown was fringed. However, these blue fringe pantsuits designed by Michael Travis, and worn here by Cindy, Jean and me, were made on a satin base underlining, which was stronger, and held up better.

Cindy, Jean, and I loved dancing in these pantsuits designed by Michael Travis, and we wore them for a medley of songs that included “Loving Country” on *This is Tom Jones* (1970). Unsurprisingly the fringes used to get caught up whenever we wore them and were very hard to untangle. Because the fringes were sewn on to lightweight sheer fabric, the outfits are sadly not now in good condition. One is in tatters, just strings and beads.

chart in *Billboard*. At the same time, our television schedule included guest starring on *The Barbara McNair Show*, *The Merv Griffin Show*, *The Andy Williams Show*, *The Glen Campbell Goodtime Hour*, and the special *This is Tom Jones*. We again had great people in promotion, who used to take us to all of the television shows and the radio stations in Hollywood.

On August 12, 1970, we were in New York City to headline our own outdoor concert as part of the Schaefer Music Festival in Central Park. It was an absolutely magical evening. We were wearing Stephen Burrows short, tight, sexy dresses. We were sans wigs, and wore our own hair, pulled up in tight buns. The fans came out—thousands of them—to see what The "new" Supremes were all about, and we were eager to show them.

This was a very exciting time for all of us. Cindy had fallen in love, and she and Charles Hewitt were married while we were on tour in the West Coast. We were all there, and *Jet* magazine ran a lovely photograph of us at the wedding.

When Frank Wilson was assigned to be the lone producer of our second album, *New Ways But Love Stays* (1970), I was thrilled. When he let me hear "Stoned Love" (1970), I nearly screamed with joy. I couldn't believe this track. From the very beginning, that song was the star of the album. In fact, *New Ways But Love Stays* was full of wonderful songs that directly spoke about a higher consciousness. My idea was to have the front cover as a black background with just our faces and our new Afro hairstyles dominating the design. The 1970s were off to a good start, being a decade of "black pride" and great social change. It was the decade of "Black is Beautiful," and we were right in the middle of it.

The title "Stoned Love" brought with it a certain controversy; we were singing about universal love, not "getting stoned." Unfortunately, my idea for the album cover was shelved. The original image I wanted to dominate the cover was relegated to the middle of five other pictures of us. I fought to keep my original "black pride" concept intact. However, I realized I had no power. That is when I decided to take over more control of the group, and I started to challenge Motown on the ownership of the name "The Supremes." I also hired an accountant, and lawyers of my own.

The new craze in music was computers and synthesizers, so Frank updated our sound with special effects. One of my favorite songs was our version of Paul Simon's "Bridge Over Troubled Water" (1970). The song was arranged so that I started, then Cindy had some solo lines, followed by Jean. It was one of the most musically lush arrangements we had experienced in a while.

Both "Stoned Love" and "Time To Break Down" introduced several new dimensions to our music. "Together We Can Make Such Sweet Music" (1970) was a declaration, and The Beatles' "Come Together" (1969) proved that we could still rock 'n' roll as well as deliver ballads and soulful tunes. And, our cover of Steam's "Na Na Hey Hey Kiss Her Goodbye" (1969) was so fun. In my mind, the music on *New Ways But Love Stays* represents some of the best and finest work that The Supremes did in this era.

"Stoned Love" exploded on the radio from the minute it was released. It became our second Top 10 hit of the year. It was exciting, it was edgy, it was slightly controversial, and it was 100% Supreme! On the U.S. R&B chart, it reached No. 1 to become our thirteenth chart topper!

Previously, we had recorded four albums with The Temptations. Now came the first of three albums with The Four Tops. It was titled *The Magnificent 7* (1970), and it was sheer fun. The biggest hit on the album was our recording of "River Deep, Mountain High" (1970), which flew up the charts to No. 14 in the U.S.A. and No. 11 in the U.K. Although this song is most closely associated with Ike & Tina Turner, our version was the higher ranking one. It was produced by Nick Ashford and Valerie Simpson, who were great at vocal arrangements. Levi Stubbs and Jean Terrell duetted on this song, and it was like watching two artists vocally painting a masterpiece.

The Supremes were still able to create hits, play sold-out concerts, and entertain millions of people on television around the world. I cannot thank Jean and Cindy enough for the work they did to make this happen. The fans stuck with us, and we were able to show the world that The Supremes could definitely change with the times. This particular year, we released three albums, scored four Top 40 hits, two Top 10s, and a No. 1 hit. We were still the biggest selling female singing group in history, and it felt wonderful to know that in our new configuration we were still viable hit-makers. I was now beginning to feel more confident.

As the new year started, we guest starred on *The Mike Douglas Show,* and on *The Flip Wilson*

Show we performed a medley of "Time To Break Down" and "Stoned Love." We not only sang on Flip's show, but we also did comedy skits with him. I loved to watch him create his comical characters. On March 6—my birthday—we were guests on *The Pearl Bailey Show* performing "River Deep, Mountain High" and Elton John's "Border Song." That month, we headlined at the Elmwood Casino in Windsor, Canada. Then it was off to Las Vegas to perform at The Frontier. I thought of Flo a lot during this engagement.

Our next single, "Nathan Jones"(1971), was released on April 15, and it became one of The "new" Supremes greatest hits. "Nathan Jones" has more of an African rhythm, which makes it difficult to perform, and most bands find it awkward to play. I rarely sing it because of that, but it is still one of my favorites.

In June, our third '70s Supremes album, *Touch* (1971), was released, produced by Frank Wilson. *Touch* had many great highlights on it, in addition to our Top 10 hit "Nathan Jones." The song "Touch" was released as a single in 1971. It was a duet between Jean and me. I was thrilled to later learn that Frank specifically wrote this song for me and my voice. When Frank brought me the demo recording of it, the instrumentation was so lush and beautiful that I knew it was finally time for me to step into the spotlight and feel confident about singing out front! I have to admit, "Touch" showed me "it's my turn!" I am so identified with the song to this day, that I use "Touch" as my salutation whenever I sign my correspondence.

The beautiful thing about The "new" Supremes' album cover for *Touch* was that we still upheld and showed the glamorous image of the original Supremes. The photographer, Harry Langdon, had us softly lit and showing our natural beauty, while sporting our own hair, appearing nude. The attractive "look" of this front cover, with its colorful psychedelic rainbow, was very appealing. In 1971, *Touch* also had the distinction of being the first Supremes album to be reviewed by *Rolling Stone* magazine. They called it "an unqualified success and the final proof that The Supremes will continue!" In 2015, Rolling Stone ran an article titled "20 R&B Albums Rolling Stone Loved in the 1970s You Never Heard," and included *Touch* on their distinguished list!

Motown released *The Return of The Magnificent Seven* (1971), with The Four Tops, in July. The album cover was glamorous front and back. The classic film, The *Magnificent Seven* (1966), was a Western. So, we had the idea of dressing like cowboys and cowgirls for one side, and then on the flip side we would be in the same style pose, but this time wearing fabulous gowns and elegant velvet suits. There were no stylists in those days; it was 100% our own concept. I absolutely loved those leather pants, and the seven of us look really cool on that cover.

In December, Motown released our third collaboration album with The Four Tops, fittingly titled *Dynamite* (1971). Frank Wilson had not produced our first two albums with the guys, but he joined us for *Dynamite*.

To record with The Four Tops was exciting. First of all, there was the fact that at one time I and Duke Fakir had been a couple, and in fact we were almost engaged. Also, my favorite male singer in the world is Levi Stubbs. There is nothing quite so exciting as recording and creating with someone you idolize. So, every time we were in the studio with them it was "an event." Obie Benson was quite a character, too. He was always "on." He kept everyone happy, because he had that kind of entertaining personality. Well, the truth is, he was a bit crazy so every moment with him was fun! Lawrence Payton was a master in terms of music. He was the genius and did most of The Four Tops harmonies and musical vocal arrangements. Then there was my guy, Duke, one of the greatest underrated tenor voices of all times. Duke's voice can only be heard in the background of The Four Tops, but it is always clear and on pitch like a bell.

Smokey Robinson—who had produced several of our earlier records when we were the "no hit Supremes"—produced our next album! Much to my delight, Smokey asked me to duet with Jean on what became the album's two hit singles: "Floy Joy" (1971) and "Automatically Sunshine" (1972). It was then that I realized I would have to start taking vocal classes, as singing out front was new for me. I began with well-known Hollywood teachers, like Seth Riggs, and "the maestro" Giuseppe Belestriarre, whom I stayed with throughout the 1970s. Needless to say, he really helped me to grow as a singer. I am to this day still taking vocal lessons. My teacher now is one of my backing vocalists, Lucy Shropshire, who teaches in the same way that Giuseppe did.

We ushered in 1972 with two Top 10 hits, "Floy Joy" and "Automatically Sunshine." We also had

This iconic portrait appears on the front cover of the album *New Ways But Love Stays*, released in 1970. It was the era of "Black is Beautiful."

Below and bottom: Jean, Lynda and I are wearing the famous Michael Travis-designed "Green Swirls" gowns for a playful photo shoot in a Hollywood park (1972).

a Top 40 hit with "Your Wonderful Sweet Sweet Love" (1972). After recording for ten years, I was beginning to feel confident as a lead singer as I was on two of our back-to-back Top 10 hits!

It was the confirmation that I needed to step further into the forefront of the group. My solo spotlight ballad on the *Floy Joy* (1972) album was "A Heart Like Mine." With Smokey producing us, it was like our relationship had come full circle in the past decade. I thank him for helping me move forward in my career again.

As we were preparing the *Floy Joy* album for release, Cindy came to me with news that was both good and bad. The good news was that she was pregnant, and the bad news was that she wanted to leave The Supremes. Oh no, not again! Either I had to find another Supreme, or end the group. I was very unhappy to see Cindy go, but there was no drama there.

Cholly, our choreographer for a decade, told me about Lynda Laurence, who was one of Stevie Wonder's background singers. I asked her if she would join us. Without missing a beat, we started rehearsing and taking photos for the new album.

In the July 29, 1972, issue of *Billboard* magazine a review of our live act stated, "The current Supremes (Lynda Laurence, Jean Terrell, and Mary Wilson) are a more open, individual act than in the past. There are more solo opportunities, while their sound retains its harmonic strength." This was a nice affirmation that The Supremes were on the right track! However, it was obvious that we needed a new direction, because the music industry and the times were changing fast.

One of the most interesting singer/songwriters at the time was Jimmy Webb. He had been a staff writer at Motown in the 1960s. Wayne Weisbart, our manager at Motown at the time, brought me the idea of Jimmy producing The Supremes. I loved it. Working with Jimmy could be a career-changing move for the group. He was wonderful to work with, and I enjoyed what he brought to us musically. Jimmy gave me a beautiful ballad as my solo,"I Keep It Hid." Although it got great reviews, *The Supremes Produced and Arranged by Jimmy Webb* (1972) was not a big hit.

Now we faced a whole new dilemma. The Motown machinery was slacking off, and Berry had washed his hands of us. Sadly, The Supremes—and many of the Motown recording artists—were not receiving sufficient support and exposure from the record company anymore.

In 1973, when we recorded the song "Bad Weather," produced by Stevie Wonder, I thought it would be a huge hit single for us. Motown did nothing to promote it, though, and it barely made the charts in the U.S.A., but it was a hit in the U.K.

Both Jean and Lynda came to me and announced that they wanted out of the group. Now that they were on the inside, they very clearly saw what I had been dealing with just to keep the group going. In fact, Jean and Lynda wanted me to leave the group and Motown, too. Now what was I going to do? We still had a calendar full of bookings for The Supremes, and two-thirds of the trio had left me!

The first person I thought about was Cindy Birdsong. She had given birth to her son, and she was back in shape. Much to my relief, she was ready to rejoin the group. The fans loved her, and many of them thought of her as an original member. Now I just needed a third singer. Lamont Dozier recommended Scherrie Payne, Freda Payne's sister. When I phoned Scherrie in Detroit, she was very excited; I sent her a plane ticket and we started rehearsals the moment she arrived. One thing that had to be done, though, was that some of our gowns had to be shortened to fit Scherrie. The Supremes were ready to deliver what made us great in the first place. Scherrie wanted to prove herself to the fans, and Cindy had a newfound energy and excitement. This made me more determined than ever to continue.

What a strange and interesting year 1973 was. Diane and I rarely saw each other, but one day we went shopping in Beverly Hills. I was saddened by the fact that Diane and I were no longer the close friends we once were. I also spent time with Flo in Detroit, which was very depressing. Our lives had taken such extremely different directions.

Now that I had taken over The Supremes' business affairs—attorneys, management, and public relations—I had my own "team." I was spending hundreds of thousands of dollars in legal fees. I vowed that I would move forward with confidence, as Mary Wilson.

Behind the scenes, though, I found myself battling with Motown over The Supremes trademark. While my legal problems with Motown soared, I declined signing the renewal of my contract with the label. In terms of recording, this meant that we were temporarily in limbo. This resulted in a two-year gap between the release of "Bad Weather" and our next single.

I was especially happy to have Cindy and Scherrie by my side on New Year's Eve at the Contemporary Hotel at Disney World in Florida. I remember singing The O'Jays' hit "Love Train" (1972) at midnight, as 1974 began, and I felt a revitalized energy about my life, and about The Supremes. But I also knew that I had to make a move soon, which was my New Year's resolution.

On January 23, we were the musical guest stars on *The Sonny & Cher Comedy Hour*. In February, we did a two-week tour of the U.K., and then we were booked at the Casino Royale in Mexico City. During that engagement, there was a fire in the dressing room of the casino, and nine sets of our very expensive gowns were destroyed. Some of the gowns were repaired or remade by Pat Campano and his business partner Richard Eckert.

After a tour of the Far East, we returned Stateside to play at some old favorites: the Fairmont in San Francisco and the Sahara in Tahoe, Nevada. We were again in Las Vegas, but this time at The Riviera. While there, I got married to Pedro Ferrer, and Pat Campano designed my beautiful wedding gown.

In July and August, The Supremes performed at the huge amusement park, Magic Mountain, in Valencia, California. I still missed Flo, and on one of my trips to Detroit I invited her to visit me in Los Angeles. I was very happy when she accepted, because I thought if I could get her out to Los Angeles, she would see some happiness.

I drove Florence all around L.A. to some of the spots she used to know when she was in the group. One place she got a kick out of visiting was The Brown Derby, where we had met Sidney Poitier. We had a really good time just talking. On the night of the show, it was fun backstage with Scherrie and Cindy, who were so happy to see Flo.

I called her up onstage and she sang with us that night. What a delight that was to have Flo with The Supremes one last time. When she came to the stage, fans yelled out, "We love you, Flo!" It was sad for me to see her so lost; she was not the same feisty girl I once knew. Flo was not with The Supremes anymore, but the night made her happy for a moment. Later that evening, she said to me, "Mary, I know what you are doing, but don't you see what has happened? I cannot be who I was!" Her eyes were not the same "happy go-lucky" eyes of a young girl. It was as if someone had taken her spirit from her years ago, and she was only thirty-two years old. It broke my heart to see her broken! After Flo flew back to Detroit, I had my own problems to deal with. It seemed I was always helping others but no one was looking out for me.

After my lawyers finished battling with Motown, I finally signed my new contract, and things got under way for us to record again. At this point, Holland-Dozier-Holland were doing independent music production. Although Lamont Dozier was off on his own projects, Eddie and Brian Holland were brought in to produce several of the tracks for our next album.

At long last, on May 12, 1975, our first new studio album, *The Supremes*, was released, and it was a victory. The album featured nine songs, on which I sang four leads.

A month later, we finally had a new single released, "He's My Man" (1975), with Scherrie and I singing duet. It wasn't a big hit on the pop and R&B charts, but it hit No. 1 on several of the regional disco charts, which were now equally important. The press ate it up, and suddenly "He's My Man" was being written about as our big "comeback" hit. We were one of the few 1960s groups who were able to make the leap into disco. The Supremes were back in a big way! So I thought.

Our follow-up single, "Where Do I Go From Here" (1975), written by Brian and Eddie Holland, was our next disco hit, making it to No. 3 on the disco chart in *Billboard*. It felt great to be back in the spotlight. We returned as guest stars on *Dinah!*, and we appeared on *The Tonight Show*. When the song "Early Morning Love" (1975) was released in the U.K., it was my first 100% lead on a Supremes single. It reached No. 6 on the disco chart.

Now The '70s Supremes were in need of a fresh new look and act. We turned to the amazingly talented Geoffrey Holder, who did it all for us. One of the great pieces of Geoffrey's staging involved a fantasy number in which each of us portrayed legendary figures we admired. Cindy was Marilyn Monroe, and Scherrie performed as blues star Bessie Smith. For my solo fantasy, I came on stage in a dramatic gown and tall headdress as my idol Josephine Baker. She had told Geoffrey that she wanted me to portray her in her movie.

As 1976 began, we made a great appearance on the television show *Sammy & Company*, starring my dear friend Sammy Davis Jr. Then in February of 1976 something very horrible and very shocking happened.

Scherrie, Susaye, and I are coordinated in red for this lighthearted photo shoot from 1976.

Scherrie, Susaye, and I—the last official Supremes lineup —strike a pose on my Rolls Royce in the "White Rain" gowns. We wore them for the photo on the front cover of *Black Stars* magazine (1977) and for several live performances.

Florence died in Detroit. In previous months, the *Detroit Free Press* had run a huge story about Flo being broke, then she made the cover of *Jet* magazine, revealing more details of her sad story. Sinking in a sea of depression, poor Flo's heart simply could not take it anymore. I naturally attended the funeral services in Detroit. It was good to see Diane there, too. It was—without doubt—the saddest day in Supremes history and my life.

At the cemetery, along with her family, I was one of the last people to leave. I said to Flo, "Don't worry, I will take care of everything." I vowed to make sure that no one would ever forget The Supremes, or Florence, and I have tried to live up to my promise. As I flew back to Los Angeles, I was filled with thoughts of the three of us: me, Diane, and Flo. I was extremely sad. My heart was broken.

Back to The Supremes. By now the sounds of disco were really driving the music business, and The Supremes were totally up for the task! Cindy, Scherrie, and I had completed all of the tracks for our album *High Energy* (1976), and it was being prepared as our next release, when suddenly, Cindy said she was leaving us again. Although Cindy was on every track of the album, I now had to look for a replacement for her again.

It was my husband, Pedro, who found the right girl, Susaye Greene. She was an undeniably powerful and excellent vocalist, who was also highly recommended by Stevie Wonder. In fact, she duetted with Stevie on his No. 1 album *Songs In The Key Of Life* (1976), on "Joy Inside My Tears."

Susaye had also sung with Ray Charles. While I regretted seeing Cindy leave, Susaye had an amazing five-octave vocal range, which was exciting and unique. More importantly, she brought "high energy" to The Supremes, and that was exactly what we needed at this time.

We had already recorded most of the songs for the album, but Susaye was added to the last two. When she put her high octave vocals on top of "High Energy" and "I'm Gonna Let My Heart Do the Walking" (both 1976), she absolutely elevated those tracks. I was enthused to have Susaye join us, but knew my time as a Supreme was limited.

The *High Energy* album had "hit" written all over it. Even the title song, "High Energy," hit No. 9 on the *Billboard* dance/disco chart. It started out with my lead vocal, and then both Susaye and Scherrie joined in with their leads. This song embodied The Supremes the way I now envisioned us being: three equally talented ladies.

"I'm Gonna Let My Heart Do the Walking" was No. 1 in the *Billboard* dance chart/club play list. It was a hit in gay and straight discos, and on every dance floor in between. I had wanted at least one more huge hit for The Supremes, and this was it!

We recorded more disco tunes for The Supremes' final album, and more great ballads for me. This new album was to be known as The Supremes last album for Motown, and forever. We titled it *Mary, Scherrie & Susaye* (1976). By this time, we knew that it would be my final album as a Supreme, as I had made up my mind to go out on my own. It was destined to be my big catapult to launch me into—at long last—my solo career. On September 30, 1976, Motown released the first single from *Mary, Scherrie & Susaye*. It was a full-out disco number called "You're My Driving Wheel." Then on October 10 came the album.

The disco crowd loved us, but the pop audience was somewhere else. "You're My Driving Wheel" made it to No. 5 on the disco charts in *Billboard*, which was a notable accomplishment. A subsequent single, "Let Yourself Go," was released in January 1977, and again hit No. 5 on the disco chart. It was destined to be the final new single by The Supremes.

From April 29 to May 7, we toured Germany, then we had additional concerts in Austria, Denmark, and Sweden, before we moved on to our final performance in the U.K. The U.K. had always been home to some of our most loyal fans, so it seemed like the ideal opportunity to make my final performance with The Supremes really special.

The setting was perfect for this event. The Drury Lane is a formal classic legitimate theater, complete with lush red velvet curtains and gold leaf filigree decorating the walls. I made certain that the last show featured many of The Supremes' No. 1 hits, our most memorable early 1970s songs, several of our recent disco smashes, and some specialty numbers, too.

It was an historic evening for me, and truly the end of an era. *Billboard* magazine even reviewed our performance. It was "officially" the end of The Supremes, and it marked the launch of my solo career.

It was now time to work on discovering who I was apart from the group, and the beginning of sharing my own musical identity with the world. I was ready to make that move, to "dare to dream" again.

Gowns in print

Record Mail (December 1964, U.S.A.)

Tuney Tunes (March 1965, Holland)

Ebony (June 1965, U.S.A.)

Mickyvision (May 1966, Holland)

Tele Guia (1966, Chile)

Cash Box (July 1968, U.S.A.)

Arts Guide to San Juan (1968, Puerto Rico)

Blues & Soul (January/February 1970, U.K.)

TV Week, The Sun Baltimore (October 1970, U.S.A.)

Sen Ben (1965, Turkey)

Almanaque (1965, Portugal)

Jet (February 1966, U.S.A.)

R 'n' B World (October 1968, U.S.A.)

Chicago Tribune (December 1968, U.S.A.)

Chicago Daily (December 1968, U.S.A.)

Sepia (August 1975, U.S.A.)

Black Stars (October 1975, U.S.A.)

Melodie und Rhythmus (June 1981, Germany)

The mentors

Berry Gordy Jr. Known the world over as the creative genius behind Motown Records, Berry Gordy Jr. started his career in the world of music as a songwriter. After writing hits for Jackie Wilson, he decided that the best way to get his music heard was to start his own record company. He turned his love of music into a multi-million dollar empire known as Motown Records. Berry was The Supremes' biggest supporter, and he turned us into stars.

Holland-Dozier-Holland Eddie Holland was a singer in Detroit when Berry Gordy heard him and said, "I want to manage you." Eddie released several singles with Berry producing them. Soon, however, Mr. Gordy found that Eddie's true talent was as a songwriter and record producer. Eddie told Berry about his brother Brian, and soon he was brought into Motown. Brian's main role was as an arranger and producer. Like Eddie, Lamont Dozier started out as a singer and recording artist. When he met Berry Gordy, he was still amid his initial career as a performer. However, it was soon discovered that his real strength was as a songwriter, producer, and musical arranger. The union of Holland-Dozier-Holland was one of the reasons why Motown Records was such a success. Together, they were responsible for The Supremes' first twelve No. 1 hits.

Maxine Powell Originally from Texas, Mrs. Maxine Powell was an influential person in the careers of The Supremes, The Temptations, Marvin Gaye, and all the "A" list stars at Motown. A model and actress in Chicago, she moved to Detroit in the 1950s and opened The Maxine Powell Finishing and Modeling School. She joined Motown in 1964, and it was her task to polish the stars: she was a motivator in classes of style and social grace. It was Mrs. Powell who said that The Supremes were diamonds in the rough and that they were just there to polish us. She predicted that we would one day meet with kings and queens, and she was correct! Always chic, Mrs. Powell never left her house without her Revlon number 725 lipstick: "Love that Red."

Cholly Atkins The Supremes were famous for our exciting stage act and synchronized choreography, and Cholly Atkins was the man who gave us our trademark moves. Back in the Vaudeville days, he had been a well-known dancer in the duo Coles & Atkins. He worked with all of the Motown acts, including The Temptations, Gladys Knight & The Pips, and Martha & The Vandellas. Cholly was responsible for adding the polish to everyone's acts, drawing on his experience on the stage in New York City.

Maurice King Maurice King was a show business professional who helped to shape The Supremes' stage act. He wrote beautiful "stage patter" for Diana, and all of the comic banter that Flo and I had in our nightclub act. King had been a big band leader at the Flame Show Bar in Detroit where most of the top black entertainers appeared, including Nat King Cole, Ella Fitzgerald, and Della Reese.

The Funk Brothers One of the keys to the indelible success of Motown music is the musicians who were known at Hitsville as The Funk Brothers. The sounds that these thirteen men came up with are the sounds of Motown that are still so instantly recognizable sixty years later. Finally, after years of being heard in the background of hundreds of hit recordings, The Funk Brothers had their moment in the spotlight in 2002. They were the stars of a highly acclaimed documentary about them, *Standing in the Shadows of Motown*.

Harvey Fuqua Originally from Louisville, Kentucky, Harvey Fuqua first found success in 1954 with the single "Sincerely" as part of the vocal group The Moonglows. After working at Anna Records and marrying Berry Gordy's sister, Gwen Gordy, he was hired by Berry Gordy in 1961 to head up Motown's artist development department and also to work as a producer. He was responsible for bringing Tammi Terrell to the label and for producing her duets with Marvin Gaye.

The designers

LaVetta of Beverly Hills Originally from New Orleans, LaVetta is a black female couture designer, which was a rare combination in the 1960s. After meeting The Supremes in 1966, while they were performing at the Fairmont in San Francisco, she went on to design five sets of gowns for the trio. She also designed for other singers and first ladies, and became well known for her "scarf dresses." LaVetta's designs have been sold at chic department stores, including Saks Fifth Avenue and Neiman Marcus in the U.S.A.

Michael Travis A native of Detroit, Michael Travis designed many iconic gowns for The Supremes. In 1968, he designed all of the outfits that The Supremes and The Temptations wore in their first television special *T.C.B.* (Taking Care of Business). In Hollywood during the 1960s, Travis was the designer for the television shows *Rowan & Martin's Laugh-In* and *The Carol Burnett Show*. He also designed for singer Nancy Wilson, The Fifth Dimension, and Liberace. Travis's gowns can be seen on tour as part of the Mary Wilson/Supreme Gown Collection.

Bob Mackie Bob Mackie studied advertising art at Pasadena City College, before he went on to win a scholarship to study costume design at the Chouinard Art Institute. He then worked at Paramount Studios, where he moved into television. Mackie designed all of the costumes for the second Supremes and Temptations television special, *G.I.T. on Broadway*, in 1969. He is especially famous for dressing Lucille Ball, The Supremes, Barbra Streisand, Carol Burnett, Tina Turner, Bette Midler, and Cher.

Michael Nicola Fashion designer Michael Nicola designed eight sets of Supremes gowns between 1971 and 1972, including the fan favorite white sequined dresses that I now call "White Rain." Nicola first started designing for The Supremes during the Jean Terrell and Cindy Birdsong era.

Pat Campano/Richard Eckert Pat Campano and Richard Eckert started working with The Supremes in 1973: Pat was a designer and Richard, his inspiration, was a drag performer. The Supremes first wore gowns designed by Pat while singing "All I Want" on *The Sonny & Cher Show*. Pat and Dick created fourteen gowns for the group, and even designed my wedding dress.

Geoffrey Holder Originally from Port of Spain, Trinidad, Geoffrey Holder was taught dancing and painting by his older brother. He moved to the U.S.A. in 1954, and was discovered by Agnes de Mille. Known as an actor, choreographer, and dancer, Holder is often recognized for his 7-Up soda television commercials from the 1970s, in which he held up a lemon and a lime and announced, "These are cola nuts." A two-time Tony Award winner for *The Wiz*, he designed several dresses for The Supremes in the 1970s.

Keith Holman Born in Kansas City, Keith Holman moved with his military parents to Montana, living near Glacier National Park. Keith graduated from San Jose State University with a degree in Business Management, and moved to Los Angeles to pursue his dream of becoming a fashion designer. After working as an assistant designer for Bill Whitten on numerous projects, he struck out on his own. He went on to design for a wide range of entertainers, including Dolly Parton, Mary Wilson, Diana Ross, Bobby Brown, The Temptations, Michael Jackson, Barry White, and Whitney Houston. He produced his own clothing line—Holman Harper Designs—and also moved into interior/exterior home and restaurant design. Keith Holman has received several awards, including the coveted Gold Thimble Award and the humanitarian NAACP Image Award for Black Designers, the RSMA Legends Award, and the 30th Anniversary Thriller Award.

Gowns on vinyl

"Baby Love" (September 1964, Holland)

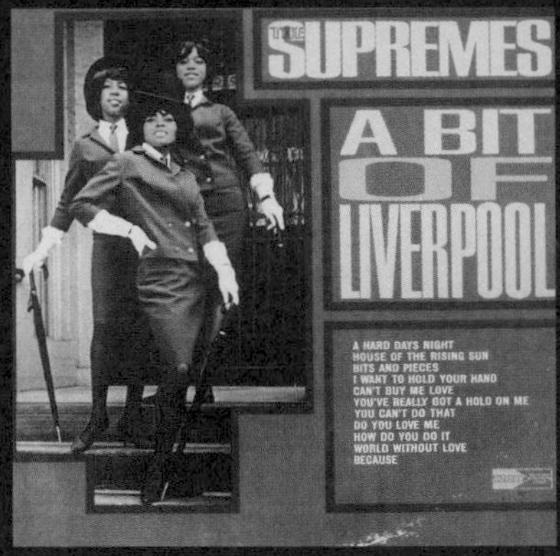

A Bit Of Liverpool (October 1964)

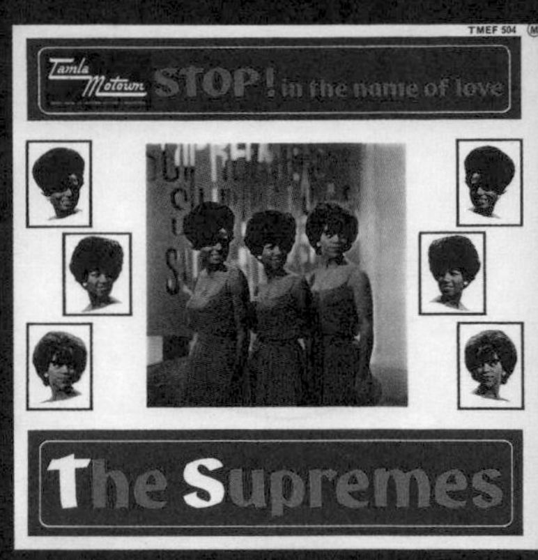

"Stop! In The Name Of Love" (February 1965)

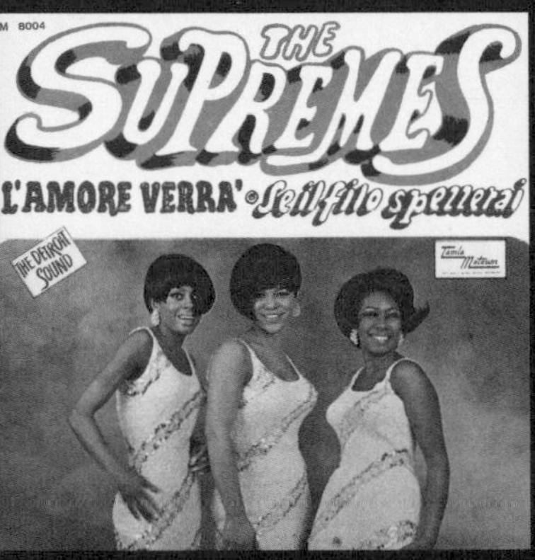

"L'amore Verrà" (July 1966, Italy)

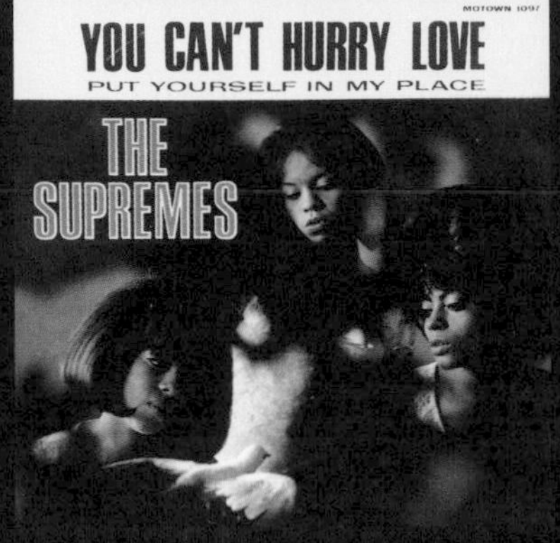

"You Can't Hurry Love" (July 1966)

"You Can't Hurry Love" (July 1966, Italy)

"In And Out Of Love" (October 1967, Holland)

Reflections (March 1968, Yugoslavia)

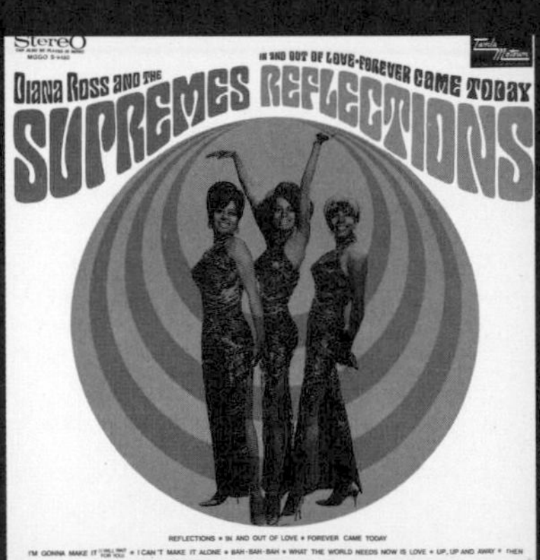

Reflections (March 1968)

T.C.B. (December 1968)

"I'm So Glad I Got Somebody" (January 1969, Spain)

Cream Of The Crop (November 1969)

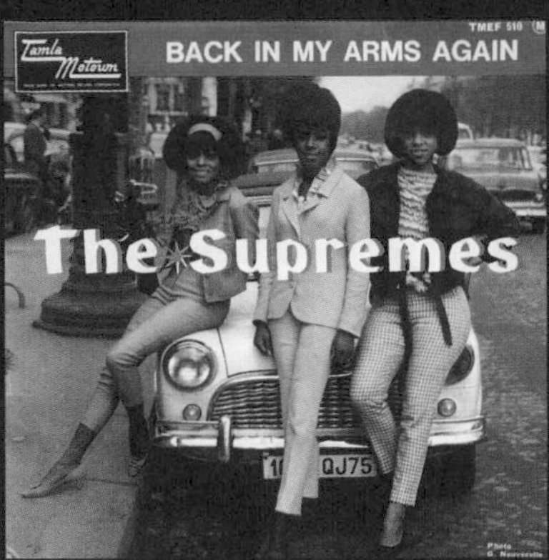

"Back In My Arms Again" (April 1965, France)

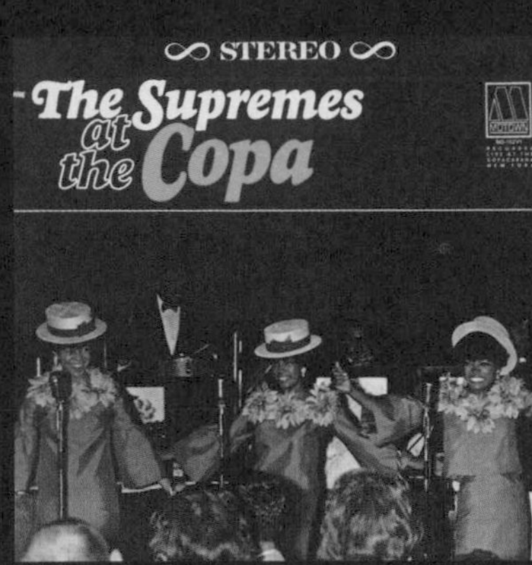

The Supremes At The Copa (August 1965)

"Love Is Like An Itching In My Heart" (April 1966)

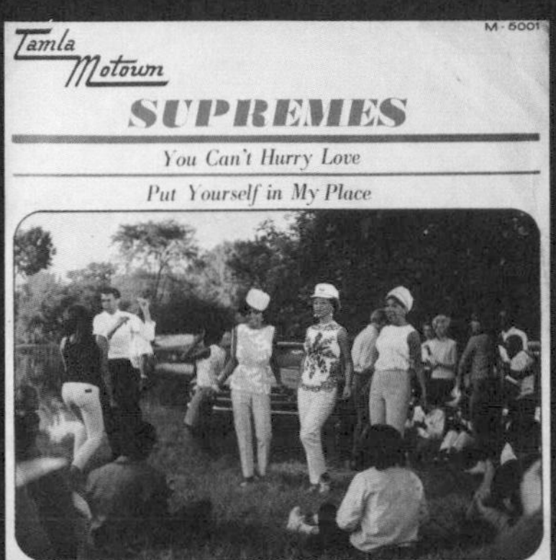

"You Can't Hurry Love" (July 1966, Spain)

"Love Is Here And Now You're Gone" (January 1967, France)

Greatest Hits (August 1967, Germany)

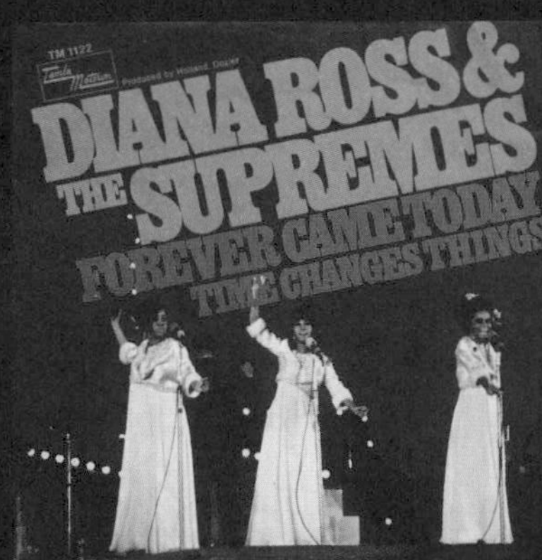

"Forever Came Today" (April 1968, Germany)

'Live' At London's Talk Of The Town (August 1968, UK)

"I'm Gonna Make You Love Me" (November 1968, Spain)

On Broadway (November 1969)

"Nathan Jones" (April 1971)

Floy Joy (March 1972, Spain)

Discography

Singles

"I Want A Guy" 1961
"Buttered Popcorn" 1961
"Your Heart Belongs To Me" 1962
(pop #95)
"Let Me Go The Right Way" 1962
(pop #90/r&b #26)
"My Heart Can't Take It No More" 1963
(pop #129)
"A Breath Taking Guy" 1963
(pop #75)
"When The Lovelight Starts Shining Through His Eyes" 1963
(pop #23/r&b #2*)
"Run Run Run" 1964
(pop #93/r&b #22*)
"Where Did Our Love Go" 1964
(pop #1/r&b #1*/UK #3)
"Baby Love" 1964
(pop #1/r&b #1*/UK #1)
"Come See About Me" 1964
(pop #1/r&b #2*/UK #27)
"Stop! In The Name Of Love" 1965
(pop #1/r&b #2/UK #7)
"Back In My Arms Again" 1965
(pop #1/r&b #1/UK #40)
"Nothing But Heartaches" 1965
(pop #8*/r&b #6/UK #)
"Moonlight And Kisses" 1965
(Germany and Holland only)
"I Hear A Symphony" 1965
(pop #1/r&b #2/UK #39)
"Twinkle Twinkle Little Me" 1965
(Christmas #5)
"My World Is Empty Without You" 1965
(pop #5/r&b #10)
"Love Is Like An Itching In My Heart" 1966
(pop #9/r&b #7/UK #14)
"You Can't Hurry Love" 1966
(pop #1/r&b #1/UK #3)
"You Keep Me Hangin' On" 1966
(pop #1/r&b #1/UK #8)
"Love Is Here And Now You're Gone" 1967
(pop #1/r&b #1/UK #17)
"The Happening" 1967
(pop #1/r&b #12/UK #6/Malaysia #8)
"Reflections" 1967
(pop #2/r&b #4/UK #5)
"In and Out of Love" 1967
(pop #9/r&b #16/UK #13)
"Forever Came Today" 1968
(pop #28/r&b #17/UK #28)
"Some Things You Never Get Used To" 1968
(pop #30/r&b #43/UK #34)
"Love Child" 1968
(pop #/1/r&b #2/UK #15)
"I'm Gonna Make You Love Me" 1968
with The Temptations
(pop #1*/r&b #2/UK #3)
"I'm Livin' In Shame" 1969
(pop #10/r&b #8/UK #14)
"I'll Try Something New" 1969
with The Temptations
(pop #25/r&b #8)
"The Composer" 1969
(pop #27/r&b #21)
"No Matter What Sign You Are" 1969
(pop #31/r&b #17/UK #37)
"The Young Folks" 1969
(pop #69)
"The Weight" 1969
with The Temptations
(pop #46)
"I Second That Emotion" 1969
with The Temptations
(UK only #18)
"Someday We'll Be Together" 1969
(pop #1/r&b #1/UK #13/South Africa #5)
"Why (Must We Fall In Love)" 1969
with The Temptations
(UK only #31)
"Rhythm Of Life" 1970 (Australia only)
with The Temptations (Australia #5)
"Up The Ladder To The Roof" 1970
(pop #10/r&b #5/UK #6)
"Everybody's Got the Right to Love" 1970
(pop #14*/r&b #11)
"Stoned Love" 1970
(pop #7/r&b #1/UK #3)
"River Deep Mountain High" 1970
with The Four Tops
(pop #14/r&b #7/UK #11)
"Nathan Jones" 1971
(pop #10*/r&b #8/UK #5)
"You Gotta Have Love In Your Heart" 1971
with The Four Tops
(pop #55/r&b #41/UK #25)
"Touch" 1971
(pop #71)
"Floy Joy" 1971
(pop #16/r&b #5/UK #9)
"Automatically Sunshine" 1972
(pop #37/r&b #21/adult #17/UK #10)
"Your Wonderful Sweet Sweet Love" 1972
(pop #59/r&b #22)
"I Guess I'll Miss The Man" 1972
(pop #85/adult #17)
"Bad Weather" 1973
(pop #87/r&b #74/UK #37)
"Tossin' And Turnin'" 1973
(UK only)
"He's My Man" 1975
(r&b #69/disco #1)
"Early Morning Love" 1975
(UK only #6 disco singles)
"Where Do I Go From Here" 1975
(r&b #93)
"I'm Gonna Let Me Heart Do The Walking" 1976
(disco singles #1/pop #40/r&b #25/dance #3)
"You're My Driving Wheel" 1976
(pop #85/r&b #50/dance #5)
"Let Yourself Go" 1977
(r&b #83)

№. 1 Hit Singles

Combined International Charts

"Where Did Our Love Go" (US pop)
"Baby Love" (US pop / US r&b / UK pop)
"Come See About Me" (US pop)
"Stop! In The Name Of Love" (US pop)
"Back In My Arms Again"
(US pop / US r&b)
"I Hear A Symphony" (US pop)
"You Can't Hurry Love"
(US pop / US r&b)
"You Keep Me Hanging On"
(US pop / US r&b)
"Love Is Here And Now You're Gone"
(US pop / US r&b)
"The Happening" (US pop)
"Love Child" (US pop / US r&b)
"I'm Gonna Make You Love Me"
(US pop in *Cashbox*)
"Someday We'll Be Together"
(US pop / US r&b)
"Stoned Love" (US r&r)
"He's My Man" (US disco)
"I'm Gonna Let My Heart Do The Walking" (US disco)

Albums

Meet The Supremes 1963
(UK #13)
Where Did Our Love Go 1964
(pop #2/r&b #1)
A Bit of Liverpool 1964
(aka *With Love (From Us to You)*)
(pop #12/r&b #5)
Sing Country Western & Pop 1965
(pop #21/r&b #5)
More Hits By The Supremes 1965
(pop #6/r&b #2)
We Remember Sam Cooke 1965
(pop #75/r&b #5)
At The Copa 1965
(pop #11/r&b #6)
Merry Christmas 1965
(Christmas #6)
I Hear A Symphony 1966
(pop #8/r&b #1)
Supremes A' Go-Go 1966
(pop #1/r&b #1/aka UK #15)
Sing Holland Dozier Holland 1966
(aka *Supremes Sing Motown*)
(pop #6/r&b #1/UK #15)
Sing Rodgers & Hart 1967
(pop #20/r&b #3/UK #25)
Supremes Greatest Hits 1967
(pop #1/r&b #1/UK #1)
Reflections 1968
(pop #18/r&b #3/UK #30)
Love Child 1968
(pop #14/r&b #3/UK #13)
Sing And Perform Funny Girl 1968
(pop #150/r&b #45)
Live At London's Talk Of The Town 1968
(pop #57/r&b #6/UK #6)
Diana Ross & The Supremes Join the Temptations 1968
(pop #2/r&b #1/UK #1)
T.C.B. 1968
(pop #1/r&b #1/UK #11)
Let The Sunshine In 1969
(pop #24/r&b #7)
Together 1969
(pop #28/r&b #6/UK #28)
Cream of the Crop 1969
(pop #33/r&b #3/UK #34)
On Broadway 1969
(pop #38/r&b #4)
Greatest Hits – Vol. 3 1969
(pop #31/r&b #5)
Farewell 1970
(pop #46/r&b #31)
Right On 1970
(pop #25/r&b #4)
The Magnificent 7 1970
(pop #113/r&b #18/UK #6)
New Ways But Love Stays 1970
(pop #68/r&b #12)
Return Of The Magnificent Seven 1971
(pop #154/r&b #18)
Touch 1971
(pop #154/r&b #18)
Dynamite 1971
(pop #160/r&b #21)
Floy Joy 1971
(pop #54/r&b #12)
The Supremes Produced And Arranged By Jimmy Webb 1972
(pop #129/r&b #27)
The Supremes Live! In Japan 1973
(Japan only)
Anthology 1974
(pop #66/r&b #24)
The Supremes 1975
(pop #152/r&b #25)
High Energy 1976
(pop #42/r&b #24)
Mary Scherrie & Susaye 1976
At Their Best 1978
20 Golden Greats 1978
(UK only #1)

№. 1 Hit Albums

Combined International Charts

Where Did Our Love Go
(US r&b)
I Hear A Symphony (US r&b)
Supremes A' Go-Go (US Pop / US r&b)
Supremes Sing Holland-Dozier-Holland (US pop / US r&b)
Supremes Greatest Hits (US pop / US r&b / UK)
Diana Ross & The Supremes Join The Temptations (US r&b / UK)
T.C.B. (US pop / US r&b)
Supremes 20 Golden Greats (UK)

All chart positions taken from *Billboard* with the exception of those marked with an asterisk, which were taken from *Cash Box*. Each position listed was the highest achieved by that single or album.

Index

Page numbers in **bold** refer to illustrations